Career Launcher

Video Games

Career Launcher series

Career Launcher

Video Games

Lisa McCoy

An imprint of Infobase Publishing

Career Launcher: **Video Games**

Checkmark Books
An imprint of Infobase Publishing
132 West 31st Street
New York NY 10001

Library of Congress Cataloging-in-Publication Data

McCoy, Lisa.
    Video games / Lisa McCoy ; foreword by Ed Dille.
        p. cm. — (Career launcher)
    Includes bibliographical references and index.
    ISBN-13: 978-0-8160-7960-5 (hardcover : alk. paper)
    ISBN-10: 0-8160-7960-9 (hardcover : alk. paper)
    ISBN-13: 978-0-8160-7982-7 (pbk. : alk. paper)
    ISBN-10: 0-8160-7982-X (pbk. : alk. paper)
1. Video games—Vocational guidance—Juvenile literature. I. Title.
    GV1469.3.M384 2010
    794.8—dc22

                                                            2009051280

Checkmark Books are available at special discounts when purchased in bulk quantities for businesses, associations, institutions, or sales promotions. Please call our Special Sales Department in New York at (212) 967-8800 or (800) 322-8755.

You can find Ferguson on the World Wide Web at http://www.fergpubco.com

Produced by Print Matters, Inc.
Text design by A Good Thing, Inc.
Cover design by Takeshi Takahashi
Cover printed by Art Print Company, Taylor, PA
Book printed and bound by Maple Press, York, PA
Date printed: July 2010

Printed in the United States of America

10 9 8 7 6 5 4 3 2 1

This book is printed on acid-free paper.

Contents

Foreword

When I began in this business a quarter century ago, it was big business in terms of potential dollars to be made, but it was also very much an immature industry comprised of a rag-tag collection of smart folks who brought their skills from other businesses to this emerging market. Even though many visionaries touted the promise of interactive entertainment, no one realized it would develop into as pervasive a form of entertainment as it has become quite so quickly. Today, the video game industry has topped Hollywood's revenues for nearly a decade running. In practice, the industry hasn't proven itself to be fully recession proof but certainly recession resistant. For those of you who are buying this book to look for ways to break into the games business in the current economic climate, please allow me a moment to give you a sense of what that climate is like and why.

Every day for the last quarter of 2008 there was news of studio closings, layoffs, and reduced publishing budgets, while at the same time hardware and software sales were up as much as 22 percent, according to some sources. Consumers are definitely "nesting," and that works in our favor, as does the fact that games represent one of the best entertainment values per hour of all media forms. Why then, one asks, does everyone seem to be feeling a pinch? And when can we reasonably expect it to end? Even more important, what can we do to make sure we are still there when it does?

To reach reasonable conclusions to any of these questions, it pays to understand the normal cycle of our industry and how that cycle can be disrupted by external factors.

The video game industry has the unique characteristic of being both seasonal and cyclical. With respect to the seasonal nature of the industry, the two major selling seasons are summer and Christmas, much like the movie industry. To have product ready for these seasons, development must begin anywhere from one to two years prior to the projected on-sale date and, for some AAA titles, even sooner. Some platforms allow shorter development timelines, but these are reasonable benchmarks for our analysis.

Because of this timing, retailers had no shortage of product in 2008 for either of the key quarters, as all of that product had been funded and developed before the gyrations of the financial markets began in earnest. In fact, there was a glut of product, particularly for the Nintendo platforms and, to a lesser extent, the Xbox 360. Whenever the market gets flooded with product, irrespective of other factors, it leads to some consolidation. Mid-tier and smaller publishers can't market their products as effectively as the larger publishers and also lack the leverage the larger publishers have in getting their slates on the shelf.

In this environment, overall sales may be healthy and even growing, but the winning titles are typically concentrated in fewer hands. For Christmas 2008 and early 2009, external factors exacerbated the normal cycle because of vast contractions in the retail sector as a whole. Declining market caps in the publicly traded publishers, grossly reduced marketing budgets, and the evaporation of lines of credit all had a trickledown effect on all the supporting players in outsourcing and independent game development. Sounds pretty bleak, right? Well, this is only half the story.

The second half becomes clearer when one understands the cyclical nature of our industry. Microsoft, Nintendo, and Sony typically release new consoles every five to six years. Each release needs good content support in order to maximize sell-through of the hardware during the first two years. To do this, publishers invest a good chunk of revenue from the last couple of years of the current generation software titles into research and development for the new platforms. Launch titles sell well typically because there is limited choice for consumers during the first year of a platform, which eases considerably during year two.

Years three and four of a platform life cycle are typically when publishers make their greatest profits as the installed base for a given platform reaches mass levels but the price point for individual titles remains high. This is also the time when mid-tier publishers flourish by offering lower-price alternatives to the AAA releases, which consumers snap up and play through while they are waiting on the next installments of their favorite AAA franchises.

In years five and six, the glut of available product and anticipation of the upcoming next generation hardware releases combine to drive down price points, and therefore margins across the board. This is occurring at the same time publishers need to begin investing in titles that support the upcoming hardware releases. In this particular cycle, the economic downturn coincides with the point when publishers are supposed to be making their biggest profits and putting their war chest to work preparing for the upcoming hardware.

More bad news, right? Well, not entirely, as there is another piece of the puzzle to examine. Publishing entities have undergone another cycle of expansion and contraction naturally and repeatedly throughout the history of our industry. When market capital and balance sheets are high, publishers almost always go on merger-and-acquisition binges. They suck up the best and brightest independent development teams and capture more of their production capacity in-house. Very often this is to capture and control franchise-level intellectual properties that the independent developer owns, and therefore recapture royalty streams directly back to their bottom line. Once acquired, these studios are often asked to perpetuate the same IP beyond their own appetite to do so, which can lead to staleness, retention issues, reduced sales, or simple erosion of the creative entrepreneurial spirit that made the studio a great acquisition target in the first place.

EA learned this last point the hard way with Westwood Studios and other former independents. When EA took over Westwood in 1998, over 200 Westwood employees abruptly quit in fear of a loss of their creative control. CEO John Riccitiello made a big point about EA's commitment to not repeat those mistakes following their acquisition of Bioware/Pandemic. This cycle of inorganic growth continues until operating costs either threaten or exceed profits for a period of time; then publishers begin closing or selling off some of those same studios. This outpouring of talent to the independent development community both reinforces the rosters of existing independents and also recombines into new independent development studios. Publishers with reduced capacity use external resources more, and as margins and profits improve again, the whole cycle repeats itself.

The major difference between how this cycle plays out normally and how it is playing out this time is one of scope. Typically, this cycle plays out in individual publishers at different times, and there are always suitors in the wings with better results ready to snap up bargains and/or immediately act as publishers for newly formed independents. In today's climate, many independents have already had to lay off some personnel because publishers unexpectedly cancelled existing projects or found themselves unable to pay milestones on time. As such, much of the recently freed-up talent won't immediately find homes in existing studios. As for newly combined studios, where a fresh sense of enthusiasm and team dynamics lend a willingness to land new projects, the situation is amplified by having many more risk-adverse publishers than normal.

Now things just sound desperate, right? When you put all of these trends together, it seems like the "perfect storm," but, in reality, the horizons are already clearing. Fear and paranoia are already being overcome by market reality, and the sheer inertia of our $50-billion market propels us forward. Interactive entertainment is not going away and too much has been invested already to allow it to languish in uncertainty in the selling seasons to come.

The scramble for development resources and talent has begun again in earnest. Expect more conservative production budgets than may have been the case a year ago, though developers who have reinvested in their engine technology and process efficiencies should have no issues with the temporarily reduced margins on individual projects. At the same time, increased digital distribution capacity is easing some of the dependency on traditional retail channels at precisely the right time. Hardware manufacturers should still seriously consider lowering their third-party manufacturing costs, as well as their digital distribution royalties in order to buttress third-party research and development investment in anticipation of the next platform transition.

What does all this mean to someone like you who is on the hunt for a job in game development? First and foremost, for the immediate future it is going to be more difficult than normal, and normal is already tough, because there is an over-abundance of experienced development talent on the market. Don't lose faith, and be a little more open to taking jobs on the periphery of the industry to build your experience base while still continuing to network and build relationships with the core industry you are targeting. Make the most of Web sites like Getin2Games.com and other resources that help you get your portfolio in front of the right folks. Go to shows, rub shoulders, volunteer your "spare" time to work on mods or other projects that get your name out there, and begin building your reputation. The games industry is a small business that is very relationship-driven. The greatest mistake you can make is to stay walled within your academic tower until graduation and believe that the sheer weight of the piece of paper you have earned should mean there is a job waiting for you. Good things come to those who work, not those who wait, and opportunities are created, not found. Network incessantly and be ready to prove your value, not just expect others to assume it as a given. Assume everyone else has talent, and that is just the starting point; work ethic is the next differentiating factor, then attitude, and finally reputation, which is the result of all of these factors over time. Your reputation is yours and yours alone to create and maintain. Guard it jealously and be proud of the you that YOU are creating, and eventually others will be as well. We hope you find this book a helpful step on that journey, and good hunting!

Ed Dille
CEO, FOG Studios, Inc.

Acknowledgments

The author would like to gratefully acknowledge the following people for their eager willingness to share their experience and insights—their help was truly invaluable and made this a much better book than I could have anticipated: Richard Rothschild, Jeff Galas, David Andrews, Ed Dille, Max Petrov, Irina Strelnikova, Todd Macintyre, Harry Pehbianto, Sunarto, Losmanto, Wendra Alamanda, Budianto Chen, Ramadona Samita, and Stan Miskiewicz. If I have forgotten anyone, know it was not intentional.

Introduction

Remember *Pong*? The little blocks that bounced the cursor around the screen...an electronic version of ping-pong. What about *Space Invaders*, with its army of blocky aliens steadily marching down the screen, intent on destroying the earth? Or maybe your earliest video game memory does not go back quite so far. Perhaps you have fond memories of Mario leaping over barrels with determined gusto as he battled Donkey Kong to reach his girlfriend. Or maybe your introduction to video games came even later. Perhaps your introduction came in the form of *Myst, Call to Duty, Halo,* or *World of Warcraft*. You were born to undertake mythic quests and heroic adventures, and you do it better than most.

Gaming is the world's oldest activity, and what makes it so unique is the social aspect. Ed Dille, founder and CEO of FOG Studios, says that, at its heart, a game is simply a structure of rules around which people interact. While this definition seems simple enough, the industry that eventually grew up around this concept is vast. In the early days, video gaming was a solitary activity, a characteristic that was anomalous with the basic, inherent nature of games. Gaming is solitary no longer. Nor should it be. Video games allow us to forge friendships, build teams, hone valuable skills, and perhaps learn a little about ourselves in the process.

Career Launcher *Video Games* will teach you everything you need to know about this exciting, ever-changing industry. It is designed for people who are entering the video game industry and will provide everything you need to know to succeed in this field, from basic concepts and terminology, to information about current "hot" areas and possible future trends, to statistics on employment and what to do to advance your career.

This book is divided into six chapters. You can read the book in its entirety, or jump to the chapters that provide the information you need at the moment. Chapter 1 provides a snapshot history of the industry, from its beginnings to the present. This chapter is designed to acquaint readers with the full scope of the video game industry— its origins, noteworthy figures in its history, where it is been, where it is going, and what drives it today. A brief chronology of this industry is also provided. Established professionals will help you understand how the industry's past is shaping its future.

Once you have a general idea of the history of video games, chapter 2 provides a detailed overview of the current state of the industry. The different types of games are discussed, from strategy and first-person shooters to card and puzzle-type games. The evolution of the technology of video games is also examined, from the arcade to the console to the PC. Select companies and individuals are highlighted, with information on the unique role they have played in shaping the industry. Future trends in the application of video games are also examined, such as military, medical, and educational uses. In addition, some of the key conferences and industry events that can have a vital impact on your career are described. Participation in these can help move a career in video games forward. Not only is there knowledge to be gained, but there are connections to be made ...connections that may put you in touch with just the right person to help you advance your career. This chapter ends with an exploration of violence and video games. Do they actually cause a person to become more violent? Is it possible to become addicted to video games? And where does *Second Life* fit into all this?

Building on this information about the video game industry as a whole—its history, its current state, and its possible future—chapter 3 provides a detailed, alphabetical listing of key jobs and positions within this industry and how they coordinate with each other. It is a glossary of sorts, defining the roles of people in different departments that are common to most companies in the industry, regardless of size. Understanding the links between positions and levels can reveal paths to career advancement, so this chapter will describe how skill sets for certain positions can overlap and lead to promotion. Of course, every individual is different and career paths can vary widely—people often start in one area and end up in a different one than they had envisioned. This chapter will provide guidelines so that people new to the field of video games understand not only their position, but also other positions and the roles everyone plays to keep the business moving. This knowledge, in turn, can help when planning the possible directions of a career in this industry.

Chapter 4 provides a wealth of information on how to thrive and succeed in this industry. Everyone likely knows the importance of not lying on your résumé, conducting themselves in a professional manner, the basics of interviewing, and so on, but, more specifically, how is success in the video game industry achieved? This chapter provides the dos and don'ts you need to know to move up the ladder and how to approach your career to best move it forward. There are guidelines for what to consider when switching from one company to another, how to communicate effectively, how *not* to land that important interview, and more. Tips on how to establish a professional reputation— and mistakes that can ruin it—are also included. This chapter also addresses the important issue of the long hours often associated with working in this industry—and how to survive them.

Chapter 5 offers an in-depth guide to industry jargon, key terminology, industry-specific phrases and concepts, and general business terms. Practically every field has terminology that is specific to it, and this one is no exception. After reading this chapter, you will know how to talk like a pro—just remember the importance of reining in the temptation to use jargon and technical terms with "non-techies."

While this book covers different aspects of launching a successful career in computers and programming, it cannot possibly cover everything. Chapter 6 fills in the gaps by pointing you to key publications, Web sites, books, schools, and training programs that are relevant to anyone working in the industry today. Subscribing to certain periodicals and journals, for example, or joining trade organizations and associations relevant to your specific position can provide the edge needed to push a career forward. Those who stay abreast of developments in this field move forward; those who do not quickly get left behind.

Throughout each chapter, you will find the following boxed items, which contain information that supplements each chapter:

➡ **Best Practices:** These will tell you how to improve your efficiency and performance in the workplace. Some are specific to the video game industry; others apply to a person's career in general.

➡ **Everyone Knows:** These items provide essential information that everyone in this industry should know. This information is crucial. Not knowing these things might even cost you a job!

➡ **Fast Facts:** On the other hand, if you want to impress someone in your next interview, you might toss out one of these handy tidbits of information. These items provide fun, useful bits of information that, while not necessary knowledge, may make you look good.

➡ **Keeping in Touch:** Even if you embrace the label "video game geek," it does not mean you have to act like one. These items will provide tips for effective business communication—through e-mail, on the phone, and in person—and include pointers on maintaining professionalism at all times. Effective networking tips are also included.

➡ **On the Cutting Edge:** These items discuss emerging trends and state-of-the-art technology in this industry. You may find these items helpful when considering where your particular niche lies or looking toward the future of your career.

➡ **Problem Solving:** While this book cannot possibly cover every contingency, it can describe common, hypothetical problems often encountered by people in this industry and offer possible solutions.

➡ **Professional Ethics:** Just as professionalism is important—regardless of the career you are in or how lax your boss is—so are strong ethics. These items describe an ethical dilemma and its successful resolution, with an emphasis on how ethical conduct can help build a strong career.

Yes, video games are fun. No one knows that more than the people who make them. They are a passionate, intense, hard-working group that possesses a dedication worthy of anyone who has ever set out on a monumental RPG quest. But it takes more than just a love of games to have a successful video game career. This book will serve as a companion on your career path and offer you the tips, tools, and knowledge that can help you succeed. You've launched this career, where you take it is entirely up to you.

Chapter 1

Industry History

When entering any new endeavor, it often helps to learn as much about it as you possibly can, and a career in the video game industry is no exception. Depending on your age in life when you enter this industry, you may have fond memories of your first Atari game. If you are a little younger, your first introduction to this field may have been *Pac-Man* or *Mario Brothers*. Regardless of your first exposure to video games, the history is richer—and farther-reaching—than you might think at first. To be sure, the history of video games can be said to run parallel to the history of gaming—and that is gaming in the Las Vegas sense.

Pinball Wizards

The precursor to the video game is actually the pinball machine— and the precursor to pinball was a game called *Bagatelle*. This was a billiard-type game in which players used a cue stick to shoot balls up a sloped table. The object of the game was to get the balls into one of nine cups located along the surface of the table. For reasons that are lost to history, the cups were replaced with plunger-type devices, and the more familiar pinball machine was born—sort of.

The game introduced in 1931 by inventor and showman David Gottlieb, called *Baffle Ball*, used no electricity and had no flippers, bumpers, or scoring device that are familiar components of pinball machines (players were expected to keep track of the score in their heads). It was contained in a countertop cabinet, and players used a plunger to launch seven balls onto a slightly sloped surface that was studded with pins circling eight holes. If a player managed to get a ball in one of the holes, a point value was assessed, depending on the hole in question. Once the ball was set in motion, the only way a player could control where the ball went was by moving the *Baffle Ball* cabinet from side to side. Interestingly enough, this is where the modern-day pinball term *tilting* comes from, which means to nudge the machine in order to send the ball in the desired direction.

Gottlieb's venture was successful, to say the least. At the peak of the game's popularity, an estimated 400 cabinets were being shipped a day. Others, of course, seeing the money that could be made on the simple device, followed suit with games of their own. Harry Williams was perhaps Gottlieb's most serious rival. A Stanford-educated engineer, Williams pushed the mechanical and electrical envelopes of the pinball machine by limiting the extent to which the human player could interfere with the ball's movement. His initial design was a pedestal with a ball on top. If a player tilted the machine too hard, the ball fell off the pedestal and the game ended. This design was eventually replaced with a pendulum mechanism. Again, if the player tilted the machine so that the pendulum went too far in one direction, play stopped. Today's pinball machines still have this feature. Williams also replaced the way in which the game was scored. Rather than circles of pins, his new machine, named Contact, used electronic scoring "pockets." When the ball fell into one of these pockets, a point value was assessed and the pocket pushed the ball back onto the playing surface so that the game could continue. This element is also still present in modern pinball machines.

The Devil's Plaything?

From there, it should come as no surprise that slot machine manufacturers saw another use for the pinball machine. A slot machine is familiar to anyone who has ever been to a casino—also known as the "one-armed bandit," the player inserts a coin and pulls a lever. (Today's slot machines have a button instead.) The pull of the lever causes three or more reels to spin, and based upon the pattern of pictures that appears, a payout comes forth—or not, in most cases. Slot machine manufacturers saw a way to combine pinball and gambling, which led to machines called "pay-outs." These games were first introduced in the 1930s, an era that was already sensitive to anything potentially criminal in nature, given the state of the times (think Al Capone, Bugsy Malone, Prohibition, J. Edgar Hoover, and rampant corruption).

Pinball manufacturers like Gottlieb and Williams feared (and rightly so) that politicians, responding to the public outcry against gambling, would soon call for these machines to be banned. Sure enough, states throughout the country passed laws prohibiting pay-out machines, often lumping pinball machines together with pay-outs. According to gamer and journalist Steven Kent, author of *The Ultimate History of Video Games*, New York City conducted one of the most flamboyant attacks on pinball. Fiorello LaGuardia was mayor at the time, and he held a press conference in which he person-ally demolished several confiscated machines with a sledgehammer. More than 3,000 pinball machines were seized and destroyed, and LaGuardia donated the metal scraps to the U.S. government to sup-port the war effort against Nazi Germany. According to Steven Kent, LaGuardia "donated more than 7,000 pounds of metal scraps, includ-ing 3,000 pounds of steel balls, and New York City's ban remained in place for the next 35 years."

What saved pinball and led to its recognition as a game of skill rather than as a game of chance—and hence, not something to be associated with gambling—was the addition of what Gottlieb called "flipper bumpers." These spring-powered levers could be used to launch the ball back onto the playing surface before it could fall out of play. Because players scored more points by knocking the ball back into play rather than relying on chance (and gravity), the game was not only legitimized, it was revolutionized. According to Roger Sharpe, the author of *Pinball!*, "[the flipper] was a remarkable change for the game designers and developers .... No longer was it a situation of a person passively interacting with the game; now there was true influencing and greater control from the standpoint of the player."

From Jukeboxes to Model Railroads

As games continued to evolve and the industry continued to grow, what was known as the coin-operated amusement industry broke into two sectors: one consisted of those who made the equipment—men such as Gottlieb and Williams—and the other consisted of those who distributed and operated the equipment. Amusement games could be found in bars, bus stops, restaurants, bowling alleys, and other locations. During this same period, jukeboxes were also part of the amusement industry's offerings, often bringing in more money than the games themselves. Joel Hochberg, a self-effacing man who only had an associate's degree in electronics from the New York Institute of Technology, knew nothing about jukeboxes in the mid-1950s, but when a neighbor asked him for help repairing his, Hochberg fixed it in just a few hours. His natural aptitude and proficiency with the machines quickly earned him a job at a company called Tri-Borough Maintenance repairing jukeboxes and pool tables. Hochberg said, "I never wanted to find out how to make things tick; I wanted to know how to make them tick better." And Hochberg certainly did. According to Steven Kent, Hochberg was the first engineer to place volume switches behind bars and counters so that bartenders and restaurant managers could more easily control the volume of music coming from the jukebox. Prior to this, the only way to control the volume was through a button hidden on the back of the jukebox, which was awkward to access and needed to remain hidden so that customers couldn't change the volume of music at will.

Hochberg's career continued to flourish. While he may not have become famous on a national scale, Hochberg was certainly well known and liked among his customers and peers. The pinnacle of his career occurred in 1962, when he took a job with New Plan Realty, which was planning to open the Cavalier—one of the world's first restaurants/arcades. Hochberg was hired to help build and manage the 2,500-square-foot arcade.

While Hochberg was making a name for himself as the man in the know when it came to not only jukeboxes but also arcades, a group of young men who belonged to the Tech Model Railroad Club at the Massachusetts Institute of Technology (MIT) had discovered computers and were tinkering with them at every possible opportunity. They didn't know Hochberg, but they shared his passion and desire to "make things tick better."

One of these young men was Steve Russell. Nicknamed "Slug" because of the pace with which he completed projects, requiring huge pushes of motivation from friends and coworkers to finish tasks, Russell nonetheless earned the respect of his peers when he helped a professor implement a computer language that came to be called LISP, which is short for "list processing language." One of the earliest computer languages, LISP was significant in that it was the springboard for many ideas in computer science, including tree data structures (a way of laying out data that uses connected nodes), automatic storage management (collecting memory that a process or application no longer needs so it can be reused), dynamic typing (checking variable types when a program is run), object-oriented programming (a program that is viewed as a collection of discrete objects that are themselves collections of self-contained collections of data structures that interact with other objects), and the self-hosting compiler (a computer program that can create its own source code).

Russell also became famous—at MIT and in the annals of video game history—for creating the first video game. The game, called *Spacewar*, was simple—two rocket ships dueling one another—yet it took Russell nearly six months to complete the first version of the game. It might have taken longer had not Russell, by his own admission, "run out of excuses." The game is laughably simple by today's standards. According to Russell, there were just four switches: one for rotating counterclockwise, one for rotating clockwise, one for firing the rocket's thrusters, and one for firing the rocket's torpedoes.

But was *Spacewar* really the first computer game? The question is open for debate among gaming aficionados and historians. According to Steven Kent, some believe that Willy Higinbotham, a scientist at the Brookhaven National Laboratory, actually invented the first video game in 1958. Higinbotham programmed an oscilloscope (an instrument that measures the voltage and frequency of an electrical signal) to play an interactive tennis game he called *Tennis for Two*. While it sounds like the precursor to *Pong*, the game does not seem to have gained much in the way of a following. Steven Russell claimed to have no awareness of the game when he created *Spacewar*.

Everyone Knows

The term *greenlight* (used as a verb in this context) means to give permission to move forward with a project. With regard to the video game industry, the term commonly refers to formally approving financing for the production phase of a game. Once a project is greenlit, it can move forward from the development phase to pre-production and the other phases.

Russell never made any money off his invention, but that was fine with him. In the spirit of true hackers, he had created the program just to prove that it could be done. He did not copyright his work or collect royalties from it. While this may seem shortsighted of Russell now, at the time, the computer on which the game was designed to run—Digital Equipments PDP-1 (Programmable Data Processor-1)—was not in high demand by consumers anyhow, partly because of the exorbitant cost.

The Computer Game Comes Home

Most people use the terms *video game* and *computer game* interchangeably. However, there is a difference. Technically, a computer game is designed to be played on a computer, whereas a video game is designed to be played on a display device. These terms will be explained in more detail in chapter 2—as well as how the lines between the two worlds are blurring—but in order to understand the history of the video game industry, it is important at this point to make this distinction.

If Steven Russell is credited with inventing the first computer game, then Ralph Baer is credited with creating the first video game. Baer was an engineer for Sanders Associates, a defense contractor, and had a background in radio and television design. Baer earned a solid reputation for himself at Sanders, and spent at least the first half of his 30-year career working on military projects before transitioning to work on transistor technology and microprocessors. According to Baer, the idea to invent a video game came when he was sitting at a bus stop in August 1966, thinking about "what you can do with a TV set other than [tune in] channels you do not want."

Baer started building a team, and development on the game began. In the beginning, the games were simplistic in the extreme and really not much fun. For example, one of the early designs consisted of pumping levers on a device to change the color of a box on a television screen from red to blue. But Baer and his team persevered, and with the addition of members who understood more about the value of fun these games needed rather than the value of their engineering, a game emerged. Initially, the object of the game was for two players to compete to be the first one to catch a moving spot on the screen with manually controlled dots—sure, it might not sound like all that much fun, but this was the late 1960s and computers, let alone gaming, were still in their infancy. Engineers, programmers, and the like were just beginning to grasp exactly what computers could do—and consumers were just starting to take notice. Eventually, the chasing-spot game evolved into a hockey game of sorts. According to Baer, "We put a blue overlay to represent the ice on top of the screen so it looked more like hockey ...[later we added] a blue color signal to electronically generate this blue background. ...[There were] three controls—a vertical control for moving the paddles up and down, a horizontal control for moving the paddles left to right, and an 'English control,' which allowed the programmers to put English on the 'puck' while in flight."

When Sanders Associations downsized at the end of the 1960s, Baer found himself about to be out of a job. He found that he wanted to stay in the toy business, but as a military contractor, no one paid him much attention. He approached General Electric, then Zenith, and then Sylvania. While Baer was smart to go after television manufacturers, and while these companies may have been somewhat interested, nothing ever went anywhere. That is, until someone at Magnavox heard about it. Upon seeing a demonstration of Baer's "hockey game," Magnavox was intrigued, seeing value in the idea. Deals were negotiated, contracts were signed, and by 1972, the finished product—called Odyssey—was available wherever Magnavox televisions were sold.

According to Baer, however, Magnavox "did a lousy engineering job ...upping the price phenomenally [they sold it for $100; Baer wanted to sell it for $19.95] ...[and] in their advertising, they showed it hooked up to a Magnavox TV sets and gave everyone the impression that this thing only worked on Magnavox sets." While an estimated 100,000 units were sold, it was this limited distribution to "authorized Magnavox dealers" that would eventually prove to be Odyssey's Achilles heel—and allow for another, similar game to change forever the gaming world.

The Stage Is Set

Nolan Bushnell, son of a cement contractor in Utah, was someone who saw what life had to offer and was always eager to experience as much of it as he could. He studied philosophy, engineering, and debate, and had a strong sense of fun. When he lost his college tuition money in a poker game, Bushnell took a job running arcade games at an amusement park. From there, he moved to a pinball and electronic game arcade. It was here where Bushnell first began to get the glimmerings of an idea. He studied the game business, learning how it operated, how to maintain the machinery, and how it worked. Bushnell was a huge fan of Steven Russell's *Spacewar*, having been introduced to it at the University of Utah.

Bushnell admired Spacewar so much, in fact, that he decided to try and make his own version of it. The result, however, was less than compelling: the graphics were misshapen and the program was too slow. Bushnell realized his mistake was in trying to devise a game that would work on a general-purpose computer. Instead, he designed a specialized device that was good for only one thing: playing the game. Bushnell's idea worked. Called *Computer Space*, it was similar to *Spacewar* in many aspects, from the graphics to the concept to the controls. With the addition of a television monitor and a cabinet—and a manufacturer in the form of Nutting Associates—Bushnell's *Computer Space* hit the market. And fell flat. Despite marketing efforts, less than 1,500 of the games were sold. The instructions were complex, and vendors saw little potential in it.

Bushnell was undeterred, however. He would take the aspects of *Computer Space* that he felt were good and improve upon the rest. He formed a company with Ted Dabney and Larry Bryan that took its name from a term used in the Japanese strategy game Go: *atari*, which is equivalent to the term *check* in chess.

Enter *Pong*

While Atari would eventually become a $2 billion-a-year entertainment powerhouse, in the beginning, it was just another startup occupying a 1,000-square-foot office space in Santa Clara, California. Bally, a successful pinball and slot machine manufacturer, was one of Atari's first partners. The two had an agreement whereby Atari would develop pinball machines for Bally. One of Atari's earliest employees, an engineer named Al Acorn, had a special knack for electronics. Bushnell, however, wanted to test Acorn, to see what he was really made of. So he made up a story, telling Acorn that Atari had just signed a contract with General Electric to design a home electronic game based on table tennis (or ping-pong). The instructions Bushnell gave Acorn were as follows: "The game should be very simple to play: one ball, two paddles, and a score ...nothing else." Bushnell engaged Acorn in the ruse just to get an idea of his skill level. He felt there was no merit whatsoever in the game's concept. In fact, Bushnell eventually wanted to produce something more akin to *Computer Space*—a game that was more complex.

But sometimes the simplest ideas are the best. And Acorn took the game in places that Bushnell had never imaged. Rather than just a straightforward back-and-forth game, he added a way to aim the ball with the paddles— the paddles were divided into segments, enabling a player to hit the ball at shallower or steeper angles—and the ball would start moving faster as the game went on. Bushnell quickly saw that what had started out as an exercise for his young engineer had become a fun, potentially

Fast Facts

The word *nintendo* is a Japanese term meaning "leave luck to heaven."

marketable game. The game, named *Pong*, came with much simpler instructions than *Computer Space*: "Avoid missing ball for high score." Atari pitched *Pong* to Bally, who agreed to market it on the provision that a single-player version be provided as well.

Pong was an instant hit. At test sites (select bars and taverns), people would actually arrive at the location before it opened, so eager they were to play the simple yet engaging game. In fact, more than once the game stopped working because it was filled to capacity with quarters.

Given the similarity between Atari's *Pong* and the Magnavox Odyssey—and the fact that *Pong* was an instant hit whereas the Odyssey never really went anywhere—it should not have surprised anyone, least of all Nolan Bushnell, when Magnavox sued Atari, claiming copyright infringements. Magnavox claimed that Bushnell had stolen the idea for electronic ping-pong from Ralph Baer, and they had the proof to back it up. Magnavox could prove that it had demonstrated Odyssey at a game trade show prior to the introduction of *Pong*, prior to the incorporation of Atari, even. And all of Baer's notes and patents on the Odyssey predated both *Pong* and *Computer Space*. While Bushnell's lawyers thought they had a good argument against Magnavox, despite the evidence, Bushnell knew it would cost more money than his fledging company could afford. So a deal was struck. Atari became Magnavox's sole licensee—and a relatively inexpensive one at that (in the future, companies that made similar games would have to pay hefty royalties to Magnavox). If Magnavox had been able to see just how successful Atari would become, perhaps they would have bargained a little harder or forced the issue in court.

Atari's Rise

With the Magnavox hurdle out of the way, Bushnell focused on growing his company. The offices moved to a 4,000-square-foot location and hired more workers. Atari almost failed to handle the growth of *Pong* and its explosion in popularity. The assembly process was slow and haphazard to start, and it took time to work out the kinks in the system. Not every machine that was assembled was even fit for use. But the kinks were eventually worked out, and according to Steven Kent, *Pong* was one of the most profitable coin-operated games in history. Whereas other games might bring in $40 or $50 a week, *Pong* games brought in an average of $200 a week. By the end of 1974, more than 8,000 machines had been sold.

Bushnell struggled to keep up with his company's success. He hired the best and the brightest (one of these was an 18-year-old Steve Jobs), and focused his attention on the future. Bushnell believed that as long as there were new ideas, the company would continue to grow. Unfortunately, he had his eyes a little too firmly on the future and not enough on the present. By the time Bushnell got around to filing patents to protect Atari products—in particular, the solid-state technology—*Pong* imitators were everywhere. (Solid-state technology refers to technology based on or consisting chiefly of semiconducting materials, components, and related devices.) Steven Kent states that "by the middle of 1974, computerized ping-pong machines were in every bar and bowling alley across the United States, but Atari had made less than one-third of them."

At first, Bushnell tried to thwart his competitors by coming out with a new game every other month. The problem, however, was that the games were still just variations of *Pong*. Bushnell finally realized that the answer lay outside of the *Pong* box, and in 1974, Atari introduced the first racing game, *Trak 10*, the first maze game, *Gotcha*, and other themed games, such as *Steeple Chase* and *Stunt Cycle*.

Atari's closest competitor at this time was Midway. Midway had nothing to do with designing and developing games. Rather, the company distributed games made by other companies. *Gunfight* was Midway's first major hit, and it was significant for two reasons: It was the first game to incorporate a microprocessor into the game's design, and it opened the door for Japan to enter the video game market (*Gunfight* was originally developed by the Japanese firm Taito).

Pong Comes Home

In 1975, Bushnell was determined to break into the consumer market and provide a game that could be played from the comfort of one's own living room. Given the still-widely popular *Pong*, of course that would be the game chosen to break into the consumer market. Called Home Pong, the device was much cheaper, sleeker, sharper-looking, and had fewer controls than the Odyssey but did not limit players' maneuverability. These advantages offset Home Pong's major disadvantage: It only offered one game as opposed to Odyssey's twelve.

As in the early days, Atari struggled to find a distributor for Home Pong, finally convincing Sears Roebuck that it was just the thing for their sporting goods department (toy store departments felt that at the price, $100, was too expensive). A few meetings and a few venture capitalists later, Bushnell had his contract, and Atari was processing Sears' order for 150,000 Home Pong units. Every one of the units sold, and with the resounding success of Home Pong, more competitors entered the market. The video game console had arrived.

They Came From Outer Space

In 1978, Taito, a Japanese arcade game company, approached Midway to talk about a partnership whereby Midway would distribute in the United States one of Taito's most popular games: *Space Invaders*. The game, for those too young to remember, consisted of rows of aliens eight columns long and five rows deep. They marched horizontally across the screen, continually advancing to the bottom. Players defended against the alien invasion by shooting at them from a laser turret at the bottom of the screen, all the while avoiding alien fire. While the game technically could not be beaten—players either continued until they were killed or gave up—from the first prototype testing in the United States, Midway knew they had a hit on their hands. Within the first year, more than 60,000 arcade machines were sold in the United States.

Problem
Solving

During the development of a game, a "wish list" of all the features the team would like to see in the game is created. For example, in a fantasy adventure game, the artists may want certain characters—let us say it is a tribe of elves—to look a particular way. They want the elves to be tall and thin and blue. The designers may want the elves to have particular powers, like the ability to stop time during the course of a game or return the player to a particular level. The producer wants to introduce other characters—a band of dwarves—so that this particular game ties into another game the company is selling. Of course, it is inevitable that some features need to be dropped. The reasons for this are myriad: development lags behind schedule, some features are harder to develop or more time-consuming than were originally thought, or resources (i.e., team members) become unavailable for one reason or another. Game designers need to be prepared for this eventuality from the get-go. In every design, no matter how focused and polished it is, there are always features that are absolutely core to the game and others that are less vital. Thus, during the planning and preparation process, a clear delineation is made between "must-have" features and "nice-to-have" features. That way, in the event features are dropped, it will be clear to everyone involved which ones can be eliminated without harming the product too much. Perhaps more importantly, such preparation and planning gives the developer a priority map, allowing him or her to focus on the more important, core features first and on the nice-to-have features later.

By this time, Bushnell had sold Atari to Warner Brothers and moved on to other ventures (most notably, the pizza and gaming franchise Chuck E. Cheese), and coin-operated arcade games were experiencing a heyday with the introduction of such games as *Asteroids*, *Centipede*, and *Gauntlet*. Midway was still one of the largest companies in town, next to Atari, and the two companies battled for market supremacy. When one company would release a game, the other would quickly follow suit, trying to one-up the other's release. The fierce competition was the public's gain. Silicon chips replaced masses of wires, new technology such as the trackball enabled players to have finer control over games, and arcade owners continued to rake in the quarters.

To be sure, *Space Invaders* was still a huge hit, but in 1980, a new game was introduced that bumped *Space Invaders* off its pedestal as the number one game, to be known forever as the icon of the video game industry. The yellow circle with a wedge for a mouth that ate colorful ghosts with big eyes and munched his way around the screen—*Pac-Man*—spawned a cartoon show, action toys, t-shirts, breakfast cereal, Christmas specials, and more. Pac-Man even appeared on the cover of *Time* magazine. According to Steven Kent, "the video game industry changed in the wake of *Pac-Man*'s success. Before *Pac-Man*, the most popular theme for games had been shooting aliens. After *Pac-Man*, most games involved mazes." More than 100,000 Pac-Man machines were sold in the United States, and arcades became more popular than ever. Video games were in pizza parlors, shopping malls, waiting rooms, grocery stores, and hotels. Other popular games (although not as popular) that followed in *Pac-Man*'s wake included *Defender*, *Battlezone*, and *Warp Speed*.

The 500-Pound Gorilla

The period from 1979 to 1983 is considered the "golden age" of arcade games. According to a cover story in *Time* magazine, in 1981 Americans dropped 20 billion quarters into video games and players spent 75,000 man-years playing them. The article went on to state that "the video game industry earned twice as much money as all Nevada casinos combined; nearly twice as much money as the movie industry; and three times as much money as Major League baseball, basketball, and football"—probably because video games were found in all of these locations!

Japanese companies earned huge profits during this time, especially companies like Taito and Namco, and in 1980, a 100-year-old playing card manufacturer that had expanded into toys and electronic games, was determined to get its piece of the pie. Nintendo tried to appeal to American players with games such as *Radarscope*, *Space Fever*, and *Sheriff*; however, it was a game about a carpenter, the carpenter's girlfriend, and the escaped gorilla who loved her that finally put Nintendo on the map. The name—*Donkey Kong*—was the creator's attempt to put English synonyms to the phrase "stubborn gorilla." As odd-sounding as the game was, it didn't take long to earn a following among both men and women.

The video game industry continued to grow, issuing forth games like *Frogger* and *Tempest* and the most successful arcade game in

American history—*Ms. Pac-Man*. Then, in mid-1982, it stopped. Why the business suddenly slumped is hard to say. According to Eddie Adlum, publisher of *RePlay* magazine, "We could just say that it is a fickle public ...movies got better ...[CDs] made their appearance ...we tried to freshen [arcade games], but apparently not to the point where the public would play [them] with the reckless abandon that they were playing before."

The Rise of the Console

Perhaps another reason for the demise of the arcade game was that companies like Atari, Magnavox, and Nintendo were more interested in bringing video games home—into the consumer's home, that is. Atari had the Video Computer System (VCS), which was also called the Atari 2600, and it did moderately well, selling 400,000 units in 1978. What catapulted the success of the VCS, however, was a licensing deal between Atari and Taito in which *Space Invaders* was converted into a cartridge and made available for the VCS.

In 1980, Mattel, the world's largest toy manufacturer, emerged as a serious competitor to the VCS. Their product, the Intellivision, had a newer, more powerful central processing unit, more memory, and the games had more detailed, better-looking graphics. Also, the controller—a twelve-button keypad and a disk that worked like a joystick—provided players with a more intricate level of precision in playing than had been experienced to date. According to Paul Rioux, former senior vice-president of operations at Mattel Electronics, "We sold about 100,000 units in 1980. By the third year, we did well over a million units ....[In 1983,] we did something like 3.5 million units worldwide."

The Rise (and Fall and Rise) of Computer Games

The history of the video game industry would not be complete without briefly addressing how the home PC came into being—after all, without the latter the former surely would never have come to exist.

By the 1950s, the idea of the "personal" computer was starting to take form and the realization was dawning that there was indeed a market for these amazing machines—provided the user interface could be improved upon, which is what took place during the 1960s. Both private and government-funded research projects led to the development of the mouse, computer networks, the BASIC

(Beginner's All-purpose Symbolic Instruction Code) programming language, and the concept of time sharing, among other things. (Time sharing, in this context, refers to sharing computer resources through multitasking.)

In the early 1960s, hobbyists were a driving force in the development of the personal computer. These amateurs were devoted—it was not easy, or cheap, to build a computer—and had an extensive knowledge of vacuum tubes, transistor circuitry, digital logic, core memory, peripherals, and more. The microprocessor and the memory chip replaced discrete components and core memory. As a result, computers were less complicated and less expensive—and now within reach of the average person.

In the early to mid-1980s, Commodore, a U.S. electronics company, was a vital player in the personal computer arena. The company developed what is arguably the world's best-selling desktop computer: the Commodore 64. With sound and graphics performance that were superior to IBM-compatible computers of that time, by January 1983 Commodore was selling 25,000 Commodore 64s per month, and this computer was a turning point in the history of home electronics. It had a slot for game cartridges, and a separate floppy disk drive was also available. Floppy disks were less expensive to make and held more information than cartridges, so this was the preferred medium for a time. Companies scrambled to create games for this new market.

The company that emerged as the winner during this time was Electronic Arts (EA). Founded by Trip Hawkins, a Silicon Valley businessman and entrepreneur, the company was originally a game publisher, moving game development in-house in the late 1980s and supporting consoles by the early 1990s. In 1984, EA approached basketball star Julius Irving (better known as "Dr. J.") and asked him if the company could use his likeness and name in a computer basketball game. This was the first time anyone had approached an individual sports star, and Irving readily agreed to EA's offer of $25,000 for the rights. Through Irving, another basketball legend was brought on board, and *Dr. J and Larry Bird Go One-on-One* was the result. The game was a huge bestseller, and would eventually lead to *John Madden Football*—one of the company's most consistent bestsellers and one of the most enduring sports series in video game history.

The video game industry went through a rough patch in the mid-1980s. In the United States, at least, it was considered dead. The international market continued unabated, however, and Nintendo

INTERVIEW

A Company Embraces the Future of Games

Yaron Dotan
Managing Partner, Das-IP

How long have you been in this industry? What was your introduction/what drew you to it?
I have been in the industry for at least six years. There are a lot of satisfying things in the gaming industry: coming up with the idea, turning it into a design, implementing the design into code and art, testing it, publishing it, and making a living out of it. However, there are two things in particular that I and my partners truly enjoy:

- Coming up with the idea and molding into a high-quality, innovative, fun-to-play, and practical game design.
- Seeing people play and enjoy the game we participated in creating.

Have you seen the hot areas in this industry change over time or have they remained relatively the same? What are the hot areas in your opinion?
There are several hot areas in the gaming industry, and they can change through the years. We believe that there are several hot areas at this point:

- The XBLA and PSN networks
- The iPhone
- Casual games in general

XBLA—Xbox Live Arcade—is a service operated by Microsoft used to digitally distribute video games to Xbox and Xbox 360 owners. PSN—PlayStation Network—is an online multiplayer gaming and digital media delivery service provided by Sony Computer Entertainment for use with the PlayStation 3 and PlayStation Portable video game consoles, as well as PlayStation.com. Currently, we believe that the XBLA and PSN networks are a hot area. Here we have a delivery system that allows a newly formed company like Das-IP to begin building a track record in the most lucrative market of all: game consoles.

The cool thing about XBLA and PSN is that games published on these platforms do not require millions of dollars and huge teams to develop, meaning that the barrier of entry is not as high as for AAA games. [AAA is an industry rating that refers to a game of the highest quality—it is akin to a movie being dubbed a "blockbuster."] In addition, the games are played on some great console hardware and the development budget is in the hundreds of thousands of dollars. This means that as designers, we have the opportunity to write games that are more complex and advanced than games developed for platforms such as the iPhone. Last but not least, these networks are still not saturated with thousands of games (only a few hundred), which [gives us] the chance to distinguish ourselves. For Das-IP, XBLA and PSN are a perfect beginning!

It is important to understand, that Das-IP's ultimate goal is to be able to deliver AAA game designs for big projects, work with the developers and publishers during the development phase, and assist in play testing, making sure the game is what it should be. FOG Studios first suggested this approach, and when we understood the benefits, we embraced it whole-heartedly.

What trends have you noticed as far as job opportunities? Can you predict any new trends? What developments took you by surprise?

As for trends, we believe that the gaming industry is shifting towards a Hollywood-style structure and model of work. Not too long ago, every developer or publisher had to do the entire thing [taking a game from concept to design to development to publishing and distribution] on its own. These days, more and more companies specialize in one particular area. There are companies that deliver art, companies that deliver game engines, and others that deliver middleware such as physics, vegetation systems, audio, etc. There are even companies that offer code or platform-specific optimization services. Das-IP strives to provide the industry with superb game designs and team up with other companies or publishers in coproducing these games. We believe that this Hollywood approach will become the leading approach for the gaming industry and we will see less and less one-stop-shop companies.

The emergence of the iPhone as a leading mobile game platform was quite surprising. Sure, for many years there was a lot of talk and effort to turn mobile phones into a gaming platform, but it never really caught on. In hindsight, the iPhone's technical abilities coupled with Apple's "cool factor," its ability to create hype and usually live up to it, the online App shop, and most importantly, the iPhone's large sales volume has turned it into a leader in the mobile gaming industry.

As for near future trends, we believe that we are going to see more Wii-style abilities in future gaming platforms—mainly in consoles. It makes sense, as it opens up a whole new gaming experience and new opportunities to design fresh games. Nintendo truly thought out-of-the-box with the Wii, enhancing the way games are played, and we believe that the rest of the industry will follow.

was determined to revive the industry in the United States. Many laughed at the tiny company's claim. At first.

Nintendo began its revival in 1985 with the launch of the Nintendo Entertainment System (NES). The NES was really a disguised version of the console that sold in Japan—the Family Computer (commonly called by its shortened name, Famicom). The NES came with *Super Mario Bros.*, still the best-selling video game of all time.

In 1989, the Game Boy handheld video game console was introduced. Don Thomas, former director of customer service and marketing at Atari, said of the Game Boy, "[It] is the most perfect example in the industry that you cannot be sure about anything, and anytime that somebody shows me something that I have doubts about, I remind myself that I had doubts about Game Boy, too." The Game Boy was inexpensive, lightweight, efficient, and could run for ten hours on four AA batteries. What the console lacked in sophistication, it made up for in portability. In a brilliant marketing move, the Game Boy was packaged with the game *Tetris*, designed by Russian computer engineer Alexey Pajitnov. The puzzle game's simple graphics were a good match for Game Boy's capabilities, and the console's portability meant that the game could be played quickly and easily during travel or on breaks. The Game Boy was an immediate success upon its release. In a matter of weeks, one million were sold. (The Game Boy Advance and Game Boy Micro soon followed.)

The Super Nintendo Entertainment System was released in 1990. This console introduced advanced graphics and sound capabilities compared to other consoles available at the time. In addition, the development of a variety of enhancement chips (which shipped as part of certain game cartridges) helped to keep the SNES competitive in the marketplace. The Nintendo 64, released in 1996, was most notable for its 3D graphics capabilities. It also introduced the analog stick (a variation on the joystick) and built-in multiplayer capability for up to four players, instead of the usual two. The Nintendo GameCube followed in 2001, and was the first Nintendo console to use optical disc storage instead of cartridges. The most recent Nintendo home console, the Wii, released in 2005, uses motion-sensing controllers and has online functionality, which enables it to be used for add-on services such as Nintendo Wi-Fi Connection, Virtual Console, and WiiWare.

The most recent Nintendo handheld console is the Nintendo DS, using two screens, the bottom of which is a touchscreen, with online functionalities and technical power similar to that of the Nintendo 64. The Nintendo DS Lite, a remake of the DS, improved several features of the original model, including the battery life and screen brightness. In April 2009, Nintendo released the Nintendo DSi, featuring larger screens, improved sound quality, an Advanced Audio Coding (AAC) music player, and two cameras—one on the outside and one facing the user.

Sega Comes on Board

Contrary to popular belief, although Sega is headquartered in Japan, the name is not Japanese. Rather, it is an abbreviated form of Service Games. The company was founded in 1940 by Martin Bromely, Irving Bromberg, and James Humpert to provide coin-operated amusement games for American servicemen on military bases. Sega was known for games such as *Zaxxon* and *Out Run*. In 1983, it released its first video game console, the SG-1000, and the first 3D arcade video game, SubRoc-3D, which used a special periscope viewer to deliver individual images to each eye. While Sega was also hit hard by the video game crash in the United States, the company re-emerged in 1986 with the Sega Master System. There was a fierce rivalry between Nintendo and Sega, with Sega touting the mascot Sonic the Hedgehog (from the game of the same name) as being "cooler" than Nintendo's Mario. The ploy worked for a time, propelling Sega to 65 percent of the market share in North America. However, Nintendo had the better marketers, and the makers of *Donkey Kong* and *Mario Bros.* reigned supreme, despite the fact that the Sega Master System could run technical circles around the Nintendo NES.

Sega Genesis, the Saturn, and the Dreamcast followed, but Sega just couldn't gain enough ground in the "console wars." This was not for lack of trying, and Sega did experience waves of success; however, when Sony launched its PlayStation 2, it soon became apparent that Sega was better off focusing on platform-independent software development. Today, the company produces games for, among others, former rival Nintendo. It is unclear what Sonic the Hedgehog would make of that.

Sony and Microsoft Get in on the Action

Sony Corporation is one of the world's largest media conglomerates, with operating segments in electronics, games, entertainment (including motion pictures and music), and financial services, among other areas. Sony Electronics is the largest of these segments.

Not to be left out of the video game market, in 1994, Sony launched the PlayStation (PS). The system was moderately successful, selling around 100,000 consoles, and by the end of 1994, Sony had sold 800,000 PlayStations to Sega's 400,000 Saturns. This successful console was succeeded by the PlayStation 2 in 2000, which was itself succeeded by the PlayStation 3 in 2006. To date, the PlayStation 2 has become the most successful video game console of all time. It has sold a total of over 140 million units and is still going. The PlayStation brand was extended to the portable games market in 2005 by the PlayStation Portable, for which Sony developed the Universal Media Disc (UMD) optical disc medium for use on it.

Donkey Kong was not the only 500-pound gorilla on the scene. By this time, Microsoft had come to dominate the software industry with its omnipresent Windows software. Having scooped up the lion's share of the software market, Microsoft naturally turned its focus on the video game console market. According to Steven Kent, "Sony and Nintendo may have created unique machines with proprietary operating systems, but Microsoft's renegade gamers built their console around basic PC architecture."

The Xbox was Microsoft's first foray into the video game console market, and Microsoft repeatedly delayed its release. When Bill Gates finally unveiled it at the Game Developers Conference in 2000, audiences were dazzled by the console's amazing technology. Microsoft's timing was fortuitous: the popularity of Sega's Dreamcast was diminishing and Sony's PlayStation 2 had just been released in Japan.

Microsoft hit a few bumps in the road with the release of Xbox, focusing more on the Japanese market than on the European one, even though, according to Steven Kent, Europe was unquestionably the more receptive market. However, this was balanced out by some strategic moves on Microsoft's part. In 2000, prior to the launch of Xbox, Microsoft acquired American video game developer Bungie, and the developer's first-person shooter game *Halo: Combat Evolved* was repurposed into a launch title for the Xbox. *Halo* went on to become the Xbox's most notable application, and the game and its two sequels have sold millions of copies. In 2002, Xbox reached one milestone that few people would have predicted: Microsoft overtook Nintendo to capture the second place slot in number of consoles sold in North America.

During 2005 to 2006, the Xbox was discontinued and replaced with the Xbox 360. According to press releases and articles published at the time, the console sold out completely upon release in all regions except in Japan. According to Microsoft, as of January 5, 2009, 28 million units had been sold worldwide. The Xbox 360 is currently available in three configurations: the Arcade, the Pro, and the Elite console, each with its own selection of accessories.

A prominent feature of the Xbox 360 is its integrated Xbox Live service that allows players to compete online and download content such as arcade games, game demos, trailers, TV shows, and movies. Major features of the console include its Windows Media Center multimedia capabilities, mandatory support of high definition in all games, movie rentals and game downloads from its online marketplace, and the ability to watch HD DVD movies with an add-on drive.

In November 2006, Nintendo introduced the Wii system to rival both the Xbox and PlayStation. The defining element of the Wii is undoubtedly its controller, which is equipped with sensors that track its movement in space. This allows players to use both the traditional buttons as well as physical motions to control their gaming experiences. The Wii is consistently the highest-selling video game console on the market, with over 50 million units shipped worldwide as of September 2009. Sales are projected to continue to increase as Nintendo recently announced plans to lower the price of the console significantly.

Clearly, the history of the video game industry is rich, with a fascinating cast of characters and all the intrigue, excitement, and plot twists that one might expect in an action-adventure game today. A full in-depth look would require a book on its own. Since several such books are available, readers interested in learning more are advised to check out chapter 6 for more information.

A Brief Chronology

1958: William Higinbotham creates a table tennis game on an oscilloscope screen at Brookhaven National Laboratory.

1961: Steve Russell develops *Spacewar*.

1972: The Odyssey, the first commercially available home video game, is launched. Nolan Bushnell forms Atari and produces *Pong*.

1973: Taito and Midway enter the video game business.

1974: Atari produces a home version of *Pong* and sells the idea to Sears Roebuck. Midway introduces *Gunfight*, the first game to use a microprocessor.

1977: Atari releases the VCS (also called the 2600). Nintendo releases its first home video game in Japan.

1978: Taito releases *Space Invaders*. The Commodore PET and the Atari microcomputers are released.

1979: Mattel introduces the Intellivision game console.

1980: *Pac-Man* is released in Japan. Atari releases *Space Invaders* for the VCS.

1981: Nintendo releases *Donkey Kong*. Atari releases *Tempest* and *Pac-Man* for the VCS.

1982: Atari releases the 5200 game console. Midway releases *Ms. Pac-Man*.

1983: Nintendo releases their first computer introduces the world to Mario. Sega releases its first home console in Japan.

1985: Nintendo releases the NES.

1987: Nintendo publishes *The Legend of Zelda*.

1988: Square Soft publishes *Final Fantasy*.

1989: Nintendo releases the Game Boy. *Tetris* is produced for the Game Boy in Russia. Sega releases the Sega Genesis system.

1990: Nintendo releases *Super Mario Bros. 3*; it becomes the most successful nonbundled cartridge game of all time.

1991: Sega produces Sonic in response to Nintendo's Mario. Nintendo releases the Super NES.

1994: Sony releases the PlayStation in Japan.

1995: Sony releases PlayStation in the United States.

1996: Nintendo releases the Nintendo 64 and sells its billionth cartridge worldwide.

1998: The Pokémon craze comes to the United States.

1999: Sega introduces the Dreamcast.

2001: Sony releases PlayStation 2. Nintendo releases the GameCube. Microsoft enters the console market with the Xbox, and *Halo* is released at launch.

2002: Nintendo releases Game Boy Advance, a backwards-compatible, portable system that can play games from both the Game Boy and Game Boy Color consoles.

2004: Nintendo releases the Nintendo DS.

2005: Sony releases the PlayStation Portable. Microsoft release Xbox 360.

2006: Nintendo releases the Wii.

Chapter 2

State of the Industry

As the technology that drives the video game industry becomes more complex, so, too, do the needs. Make no mistake: Video games are a business. Most companies are profit-driven and have to take not only current trends into account, but future trends as well—in addition to customer demands, marketplace needs, and more. To completely understand this industry, it is necessary to look at trends in employment and wages, where the hot areas are now and where they may lie in the future, which is a primary focus of this chapter. In addition, people new to this field can benefit from the wisdom of those who have gone before, so this chapter looks at the people and companies who have significant roles in the video game industry and also takes a look at conferences and events that could help further your career.

Trends in Employment and Wages

The video game industry employs many of the same types of people as the computing industry in general—programmers, testers, writers, and editors—but also employs people like artists, designers, producers, and composers. This section provides a brief overview of some of these positions with regard to employability and wages in general. For more specific information, readers are encouraged to refer to chapter 3. The U.S. Bureau of Labor Statistics Web site at http://www.bls.gov can also provide some help in this area, but does not contain information specific to the video game industry.

However, you can search for specific positions and glean some information from that. (A search for graphic designers, for example, will provide information on necessary training, job outlook, and earnings data. A look at the "Related Occupations" section shows that one of the arenas in which graphic designers are employed is video games.)

According to Entertainment Software Association (ESA) president Doug Lowenstein, "The U.S game industry was worth $10.3 billion in 2004, but it generated a further $7.7 billion in economic value, and the game industry was directly or indirectly responsible for 144,000 jobs in 2004"—a number that Lowenstein said would grow to 265,000 by 2010.

Programmers, naturally, are one of the largest sectors of the video game industry, and this chapter has a great deal of information on that sector. This is not to say that the other areas are not important—they most certainly are. After all, without savvy marketers, creative designers, and talented composers and artists, the programmer is just writing code that may never amount to much. Where possible, the information presented here is as it relates to the video game industry; where such information is not available, more general statistics and trends are reported on.

According to the U.S. Department of Labor, computer programmers held about 435,000 jobs in 2006. An estimated 8 out of 10 held an associate's degree or higher in 2006; nearly half held a bachelor's degree, and 2 out of 10 held a graduate degree.

Prospects for advancement as a computer programmer are good—provided one keeps up-to-date with the latest technology. This is not a field for someone who does not thrive on change and who has a hard time learning to adapt.

The employment of computer programmers is expected to decline by 4 percent through 2016. However, because computer programmers can transmit their programs over the Internet, they can perform their job from anywhere in the world, allowing companies to employ workers in countries that have lower prevailing wages (remember, video games are produced throughout the world).

Computer programmers are at a much higher risk of having their jobs outsourced than are workers involved in more complex and sophisticated functions, such as software engineering. Much of the work of computer programmers requires little localized or specialized knowledge and can be made routine once a particular programming language is mastered. Nevertheless, local programmers will always be needed. Employers especially value programmers who understand how their role fits into the company's overall business and objectives.

Despite the projected decline, numerous job openings will result from the need to replace programmers who leave the labor force or who transfer to other occupations. Prospects likely will be best for applicants with a bachelor's degree and experience with a variety of programming languages and tools. The languages that are in demand today include C++, Java, and other object-oriented languages, as well as newer, domain-specific languages that apply to computer networking, database

Fast Facts

According to an August 2007 MSNBC article, the top five most addictive video games are (in order of most to least): *World of Warcraft*, *EverQuest*, *Peggle*, *Doom*, and *Tetris*.

management, and Internet application development. As always, the computer programmer who stays up-to-date on the technology is the programmer with the edge.

Median annual earnings of computer programmers were $65,510 in May 2006. The middle 50 percent earned between $49,580 and $85,080 a year. The lowest 10 percent earned less than $38,460, and the highest 10 percent earned more than $106,610. According to the National Association of Colleges and Employers, starting salary offers for computer programmers averaged $49,928 per year in 2007.

At its heart, a video game is just a piece of software—and the users of that software must be supported should problems occur. And do not underestimate the importance of this job. If a poorly made video game is released and it presents players with too many difficulties, customer support staff are the first to hear about it. In the initial weeks after a game's release or around the holidays, some companies bring in quality assurance tests to help with customer support—sometimes even production teams have to field these calls and e-mails. Computer support specialists held about 552,000 jobs in 2006. Employment of computer support specialists is expected to increase by 13 percent from 2006 to 2016. Demand for these workers will result as companies continue to adopt increasingly sophisticated technology. Job growth will continue to be driven by the ongoing expansion of the computer system design and related services industry, which is projected to remain one of the fastest-growing industries in the U.S. economy. As with other positions in this field, the adoption of new mobile technologies, such as the ability to play games on mobile devices ranging from iPhones to BlackBerries, will continue to create a need for these workers to familiarize and educate computer users. Consulting jobs for computer support specialists also should continue to increase as businesses seek help managing, upgrading, and customizing computer systems that are becoming ever more complex, which, in turn, means that video games are becoming more complex.

Median annual earnings of computer support specialists were $41,470 in May 2006. The middle 50 percent earned between $32,110 and $53,640. The lowest 10 percent earned less than $25,290, and the highest 10 percent earned more than $68,540.

Graphic designers—the artists of the video game world—held about 261,000 jobs in 2006 according to the U.S. Department of Labor and Statistics. Employment of graphic designers is expected to increase at an average pace—around 10 percent from 2006 to 2016—however, fierce competition for jobs is expected; those with a bachelor's degree and knowledge of computer design software, particularly those with animation experience, will have the best opportunities as demand increases.

Not All Games Are the Same

Despite what you might think, not all video games are created equal. They are broken down into various categories based on things such as the nature of game play, the point of view, and even genre. In addition, as games evolve, these genres often overlap. Sports games are now combining elements of adventure games, as are action games.

➜ **Strategy-based games:** Often called real-time strategy games (RTS), these are complicated affairs, typically involving managing multiple resources and many different characters to complete a quest or fulfill some other goal. Because the user interface is so complicated, strategy games are still found primarily on the PC; there are few console-based strategy games. Classic examples include

Command & Conquer, Warcraft, and *Starcraft.* Such games may also be turn-based; popular examples include *Civilization, X-Con,* and *Heroes of Might and Magic.*

➡ **Life simulations:** Simulation games fall into the broader category of action games (most video games fall into this category, with the exception of card/puzzle games). Also known as "God games," this genre has been popular practically since computer games arrived on the scene. Simulation games involve manipulating and modeling realistic behavior and decision making in a nearly unlimited range of environments. *The Sims* series is perhaps the most popular in this genre; other notables include *Zoo Tycoon, Roller Coaster Tycoon,* and the *Caesar* series.

➡ **Shooters:** These games are also considered action games and are typically from the first-person viewpoint—hence the acronyms FPS (first person shooter) and POV (point of view) that are applied to shooter games. These are among the most popular video games for the PC, in large part due to the fact that they can be played in multiplayer mode over the Internet in networks. As the name implies, these games involve toting a gun and shooting various "enemies." Classic examples include the *Quake* series, *Doom,* and *Half-Life.*

➡ **Action:** Action games require quick thinking, quicker reflexes, and excellent eye-hand coordination. Most video games fall into this category, but the trend lately has been to add elements of adventure so that these games are not just about running around at a frenetic pace shooting anything that moves. Recent examples of this hybridized version of action games include the *Tomb Raider* series, *Max Payne,* and *Devil May Cry.*

➡ **Sports:** This is perhaps the largest genre of video games, surpassing action/adventure games in popularity. At least one out of every five video games sold is a sports game. However, these games are also the most costly to produce, given the complexities of player and league licensing, franchise rights, and programming that are involved. Players can experience the thrill of winning the Superbowl, race a Formula One racecar, fight Evander Holyfield, play basketball with their favorite legends, and more. Popular titles include the *John Madden* series, the *Tony Hawk* series, and *Dave Mirra BMS Biking*.

➡ **Adventure/RPG:** These games are a solid mainstay in the video game industry, with such classics as the *Final Fantasy* series (still the most popular series every made) and *Myst*. In these games, players take characters that are relatively weak and, through conquests and combat, build them up into stronger, more powerful characters, able to take on harder and more complex adventures. Role-playing games often have a back story of some sort—some are more complex than others. Elements of adventure games are now being incorporated into other genres, such as shooter and racing games. Other notable titles include *Zelda*, *Resident Evil*, and *Diablo*.

➡ **Racing:** Racing games have been popular since the inception of Atari's *Trak 10*, but have become harder to produce for the same reasons as sports games—the high costs associated with franchising and licensing. Popular titles include *Nascar*, *Formula One*, and *Gran Turismo*.

➡ **Fighting:** This is another popular genre in which, as might be expected, players fight opponents, whether in an arena or on the street. Most fighting games found popularity in the arcades first and then were brought over to the console. Classic titles include the *Mortal Kombat* series, *Street Fighter*, and *Tekken*.

Fast
Facts

A video game version of the movie *WarGames*, a film noted for its prescient take on the dangers of war in a digital age, was made in 1984 for the ColecoVision, Commodore 64, and Atari 8-Bit computers. The game started out greeting the player as Professor Falken and a game of global thermonuclear war would be played. The objective was to stop nuclear war from occurring by protecting the country with various military vehicles and weapons in a set time limit without reaching Defcon 1.

➡ **Platform/arcade:** Also called side-scrollers because of the linear nature of game play, these games are a nostalgic homage of sorts to the early days of video games. These classic action games include titles such as *Crash Bandicoot*, *Sonic the Hedgehog*, and *Super Mario*, as well as several Disney-licensed titles.

➡ **Card/puzzle:** While this genre may lie quietly in the background, its popularity should not be underestimated, as it is one of the most dominant in the video game industry (just think of how many people are playing *Solitaire* when they should be working!). Found almost exclusively on the PC, other popular titles include *Bridge*, *Poker*, and *Mind Rover*.

How Technology Has Evolved and Changed

When Steven Russell designed *Spacewar*, it is hard to know for sure if he anticipated where video games would have taken us today. To be sure, David Gottlieb would have a hard time seeing any resemblance to *Baffle Ball* in games such as *World of Warcraft* and *Grand Theft Auto*. And yet, the evolution of this technology seems natural, where each element flows out of the ones that came before it. As the computer industry changed and evolved, the video game industry followed suit.

Video game technology falls into the following four categories:

➡ Arcade machines
➡ Console games
➡ PC games
➡ Handheld devices

Arcade Machines

Arcade machines generally are coin-operated video games. These are free-standing, all-inclusive devices operated by inserting coins into a slot for a set period of time or a certain number of games. While most people think of classics such as *Pac-Man* and *Donkey Kong* when they think of arcade games, nondigital games like air hockey, pool, foosball, and—of course—pinball fall into this category as well. Many of the most popular titles available today started life as arcade games and made the transition later to handheld consoles and PCs. Arcade games are usually action-oriented and have a faster, more powerful processor than home video games or consoles. Some even feature specialized equipment such as motorcycle handlebars and a seat or a rifle.

It is a mistake to think of arcade games as old-fashioned or something that kids today have thrown over in favor of PC- and console-based games. To the contrary, arcade games are still popular largely because of the social element. According to Ernest Adams, author of *Break into the Game Industry*, "[Arcade games give] kids a place to go, play games, and hang around together without their parents. [They] are common anywhere that kids might be stuck with nothing to do, such as airports and hotels, and they're popular moneymakers for resorts and theme parks."

Arcade games are driven by money—to be specific, how much money can be made in the shortest period of time. To the end, game play typically lasts anywhere from three to ten minutes, and play gets progressively harder as the game continues. Called "coin-drop," this requires developers to walk a fine line: Make the game too hard, too soon and players will walk away in frustration. However, make it too easy right off the bat and players will walk away in search of a better challenge.

Console Games

As has been mentioned in this book, the term *video games* is used to refer to the entire range of games in general for the sake of convenience. However, in popular parlance, when someone uses the term, he or she is commonly referring to a console-based video game. These single-purpose devices are arguably the most popular—and perhaps the most important—gaming devices around. These devices are connected to a television set and are used specifically to play games. Examples include Sony's PlayStation, Nintendo's GameCube, and Sega's Dreamcast. As technology advances, consoles are being used for other purposes as well. The Microsoft Xbox 360, for example, can be used as a video game console and as a DVD player.

Because of the amazing popularity of video consoles, according to author Ernest Adams, "if a game exists in both a personal computer and home console version, chances are the home console version will outsell the PC version by three to ten times as much—even if the price is the same or higher for the console version. The main explanation for this is that there are simply more console machines in homes around the world than there are personal computers. A home console machine costs between $100 and $300. Personal computers cost five to ten times as much."

The early consoles could only play one game and had limited processing power and memory. The consoles of today have more power, more features, and more capabilities. They usually cost anywhere from $300 to $700 when first introduced, but the price drops as successive versions are released. Video game consoles use peripheral devices—generally a console with a joystick-type device and buttons for manipulating game play. Although technically speaking, playing a video game on a console is similar to playing it on a PC, according to Alan Gershenfeld, Mark Loparco, and Cecilia Barajas, authors of *Game Plan*, "Playing a game with a [gamepad] three or four feet from a television is a fundamentally different experience than playing a game with a keyboard and mouse one or two feet from a computer. This may be why certain gaming genres that involve complex interfaces ...have made a poor showing on the console and why more 'twitch'-oriented games ...and fighting games .. have done better on the consoles."

Developing a game for a video game console is slightly different from developing games for the PC. Because the device is not a general-purpose machine, like a PC, the programming code cannot be written on the video game console device, which is what will play the game. (This is how developers write games for a PC.) Instead, "development stations" are used. These specialized devices enable developers to write code for the game on a PC, which is then translated via special hardware over a link to the video game console.

PC Games

Unlike console-based games, PC games are designed for and played on a personal computer. Interestingly enough, the market for PC-based games is smaller than the market for console-based games, but this is still a large market by anyone's standards. According to authors Alan Gershenfeld, Mark Loparco, and Cecilia Barajas, "it is the computer gamers' thirst for better graphics, faster frame rates, and better multiplayer capabilities that not only drives chip enhancement but actually drives sales."

There are important differences between video console games and PC games. For one thing, because PC are multipurpose devices, they tend to cost more than consoles and can only be used by one player at a time (although this individual player can play games online with hundreds, if not thousands, of other people). PC games are often trickier to install and often require patches or updates on a regular basis. Because PCs are more complex and have peripherals like a mouse and a keyboard, game play can often be more intricate and complex. However, this facet can also be a downfall. PCs do not have a standard set of features across the board. Games written for PCs have to run on a wide variety of processing speeds, with different amounts of RAM and varying video resolutions. Game developers cannot possibly address every single contingency when designing a game. They do their best to address the lowest common denominator, as it were, but unanticipated differences from one player's machine to the next can make games not work properly, or even not work at all.

Handheld Devices

While at first glance, these devices might seem like a miniature video game console, in truth, they are slower, have less RAM, and have a smaller screen than their larger brethren. Games for hand-held devices are often single-player games, given these limitations, and the buttons and controllers are built into the device rather than being a separate accessory. Programmable machines, like the Nintendo Game Boy, are toys of a sort designed exclusively for game play. However, personal digital assistants (PDAs) and cell phones can be considered handheld devices that play games. The market for these games is solid and growing steadily. However, games designed for handheld devices will not have the same challenges (and likely rewards) as do the larger, more elaborate PC and console games. The advantages of handheld devices include their size and portability (they can fit in a pocket or bag and go anywhere), in addition to the fact that they are self-contained and are battery-operated.

Conferences You Cannot Afford to Miss

Conferences, expos, and trade shows are some of the best places to see and be seen. These venues provide a great opportunity to preview the latest advances in both games and the devices used to play them, explore where the technology is taking the industry, and perhaps make some valuable connections.

CES The Consumer Electronics Show is the largest of its kind. The focus is on games as well as consumer electronics in general. Of late, it has been surpassed by E3, which is aimed exclusively at gaming. However, it may still be of use to programmers, designers, and the like. (http://www.cesweb.org)

DICE Summit The Design, Innovate, Communicate, and Entertain conference is put on annually by the Academy of Interactive Arts and Sciences in Las Vegas, Nevada. While not as well attended as GDG, it is often the place to find industry head honchos. The emphasis is on the business and production end of the video game industry, with a focus on trends and innovations in video game design. (http://www.dicesummit.org)

Digital Hollywood This is one of the largest trade shows for those in the entertainment and technology industry, with an emphasis on digital media. Past speakers have included Nolan Bushnell (founder of Atari), Robert Kotick (CEO and president of Activision), Bing Gordon (former CCO of Electronic Arts), and Rob Glaser (founder of Real Networks). (http://www.digitalhollywood.com)

E3 The Electronic Entertainment Expo is one of the biggest, most important conventions a person in this field can attend. It is usually held in May in Los Angeles. This annual trade show is produced by IDSA, the publishers' trade association. While the conference is aimed at publishers and distributors, giving them an opportunity to showcase their latest games to retailers, developers often attend as well. (http://www.e3expo.com)

GDC The Game Developers' Conference is held every year in San Jose, California. This is arguably one of the most important conferences that a person in this industry—especially a video game developer—can attend. The European version is held annually in London. It combines a trade show, seminars, and networking opportunities. (http://www.gdconf.com)

GenCon Billed as "the best four days in gaming," this conference was primarily focused on science fiction and fantasy, but encompasses role playing games now, too. What began as an informal gathering of war-gaming enthusiasts in a home in Lake Geneva, Wisconsin, is now one of the largest and most prominent annual gaming conventions in North America.(http://www.gencon.com)

SIGGRAPH This annual conference, hosted by the Special Interest Group of the Association for Computing Machinery, is aimed primarily at graphics designers and animators, and the other *artistes* of the gaming world. There are also several different seminars, trade shows, and networking opportunities to take advantage of. Graphics programmers are strongly encouraged to attend this conference. (http://www.siggraph.org)

Tokyo Game Show   This video game expo/convention held in the Makuhari Messe, in Chiba, Japan, is open to the press, publishers, and developers, and allows the general public to attend on the last two days. (http://tgs.cesa.or.jp/english)

Paid to Play: Professional Competitions

While it is a common myth that people who work in video games just sit around all day playing them, it is possible to earn money playing video games—to a degree. Surely no one has gotten rich doing this (yet), but professional video game competitions can help someone interested in the field build a name for him- or herself— and make some valuable connections along the way. The arena is growing and gaining more widespread recognition. Well-known competitions include those hosted by GDFest, a Seattle-based company that organizes competitions across the country in both PC and console-based play; QuakeCon (http://www.quakecon.org), one of the longest running and most prominent local area network (LAN) competitions in North America; and the World Cyber Games, held in Seoul, South Korea (http://www.worldcybergames. com). The World Cyber Games has become the world's largest video game competition. Gamers from as many as 55 countries participate in the seven-day tournament for rather large amounts of prize money.

There is even a Major League Gaming association (http://www. mlgpro.com) with a Pro Circuit that (as of this writing) holds competitions in *Halo 3* (Xbox 360), *Gears of War 2* (Xbox 360), *World of Warcraft* (PC), *Call of Duty 4* (Xbox 360), and *Rainbow Six: Vegas 2* (Xbox 360). The top prize in the national championships for *Halo* was $100,000, so maybe it is possible to get rich playing video games professionally after all—or at least to make some decent cash. According to ESPN writer Patrick Hruby, Claude Chaisson, a 29-year-old *Rainbow Six* player from Nova Scotia, estimates that he has made about $10,000 over the last three years playing in online and in-person tournaments (although he also has a full-time job as a Web programmer).

On the Cutting
Edge

Project Natal is the code name for a "controller-free gaming and entertainment experience" currently under development at Microsoft for the Xbox 360 video game platform. Following in the wake of Nintendo's Wii and based on an add-on peripheral for the Xbox 360 console, Project Natal enables users to control and interact with the Xbox 360 without touching a game controller through a natural user interface using gestures, spoken commands, or presented objects and images. The device uses a camera to track a user's movements via full skeletal mapping. It also recognizes voices and vocal commands. According to a Reuters article published June 1, 2009, Microsoft plans to boost its Xbox 360 gaming console by integrating music-streaming service last.fm, Web social network Facebook, and microblogging site Twitter into its Xbox Live online community to help push the impetus for this exciting new venture in the field of video games.

However, this sport—for all that it basically involves just sitting in front of a screen—can be physically demanding on players. Many practice three or four hours a day, 30 to 40 hours a week (double that in the weeks leading up to a tournament), and there are the constant neck aches, back pain, shoulder soreness, and migraine headaches to deal with, along with the real possibility of carpal tunnel syndrome. Both practice and travel can be grueling for players. And then there's the fact that most professional video gamers have a shorter-lived career than some professional football players. Major League Gaming cofounder Mike Sepso doubts that anyone over the age of 30 has the visual acuity to remain competitive. So keep that in mind if the idea of playing video games professionally sounds appealing.

Industry-Shaping Forces and People

Obviously, not every influential person in the video game industry is covered in this chapter; nor is the inclusion of some companies but not others to be taken as any sort of an endorsement for these companies. The video game industry is huge—new players are emerging every day (you, the reader, could be one of these budding giants), and there are a wide variety of companies who need your talent. Chapter 6 provides more resources with regard to organizations, trainings, books, Web sites, and more.

Cliff Bleszinski

As the design director for the game development company Epic Games in Cary, North Carolina, Bleszinski is most famous for his continuing hand in the development of the *Unreal* and *Gears of War* franchises. His first game was *The Palace of Deceit: Dragon's Plight*, a 1991 adventure game for Windows. He is also known for the games *Dare to Dream* and *Jazz Jackrabbit*. Bleszinski is also known for his generous nature—often lending a hand and doing what he can to help fans get a job in the video games industry.

Electronic Arts

Headquartered in the Redwood Shores neighborhood of Redwood City, California, Electronic Arts (EA) is an international developer, marketer, publisher, and distributor of video games. The company was founded by Trip Hawkins, former director of strategy and marketing at Apple. By the early 2000s, EA had become one of the world's largest third-party publishers. In its May 2008 annual report, the company reported net annual revenue of $4.02 billion in fiscal year 2008 and employed around 2,800 people.

In 2004, Electronic Arts was criticized for employees working extraordinarily long hours—up to 100 hours per week—and not just at "crunch" times leading up to the scheduled releases of products. According to a March 2009 article on Gamespot.com, the company has since settled a class action lawsuit for $15.6 million brought by game artists to compensate for "unpaid overtime." As a result, an article on Gamsutra.com reported that many of the lower-level developers (artists, programmers, producers, and designers) are now working at an hourly rate. A similar suit brought by programmers was settled for $14.9 million.

Since these criticisms first aired, it has been reported that EA has taken steps to positively address "work-life balance" concerns by focusing on long-term project planning, compensation, and communication with employees. These efforts may be paying off. In December 2007, an internal EA employee survey showed a 13 percent increase in employee morale and a 21 percent jump in management recognition over a three-year period.

Currently, EA's most successful products are sports games published under its EA Sports label; games based on popular movie licenses such as *Harry Potter*; and games from long-running franchises like *Need for Speed, Medal of Honor, The Sims*, and *Battlefield*. They are also the distributors of the *Rock Band* series.

LucasArts Entertainment Company

This company was founded in May 1982 as the video game development group of Lucasfilm Limited, the film production company of George Lucas. Lucas wanted his company to branch out into other areas of entertainment, and so he cooperated with Atari to produce video games. LucasArts was famous for its innovative line of graphic adventure games, the critical and commercial success of which peaked in the mid-1990s. The first adventure game developed by Lucasfilm Games was *Labyrinth* , based on the Lucasfilm movie of the same name. Today—to no one's surprise—the company primarily publishes games based on the *Star Wars* franchise. However, on July 6, 2009, LucasArts announced that they would be re-releasing a number of their classic games for Windows, including *Indiana Jones and the Fate of Atlantis* and *LOOM*, on Steam (a digital distribution, digital rights management, multiplayer, and communications platform used to distribute a wide range of games and related media entirely over the Internet.) According to the company's Web site, more than 350 people are employed at LucasArts in a variety of different positions.

Microsoft Corporation

Microsoft, headquartered in Redmond, Washington, has been the target of criticism for its monopoly-like business practices, but no one can doubt the company's clout. According to the company's annual report for 2005, Microsoft's reach extends to the MSNBC cable television network and the MSN Internet portal, and the company markets both computer hardware products, such as the Microsoft mouse, and home entertainment products, such as the Xbox, Xbox

360, Zune, and MSN TV. According to the Microsoft Web site, as of December 31, 2008, the company employed 95,828 people worldwide, 57,588 of whom were in the United States. In 2005, Microsoft received a 100 percent rating in the Corporate Equality Index from the Human Rights Campaign, a ranking of companies by how progressive the organization deems their policies concerning lesbian, gay, bisexual and transsexual employees.

Best Practice

In this field, it is important to expect the unexpected. Consider all possible situations under which a game will run and anticipate any errors that could result. While these contingencies can vary widely, checking and double-checking your work can help avoid costly mistakes down the line.

Shigeru Miyamoto

Known as the "father of modern video games" and the "Walt Disney of electronic gaming," this Japanese video game designer and producer is the brains behind the *Mario* franchise, *Donkey Kong*, *The Legend of Zelda*, *Star Fox*, the *Pikmin* and *F-Zero* franchises, and games such as *Nintendogs* and *Wii Music*. Although a game designer, according to one published biography, Miyamoto actually does not spend much time playing games, preferring to play the guitar and banjo. His work style is legendary—Miyamoto has been known to have Nintendo implement delays "to make a game ... of the high quality standards that Nintendo is known for," at times even scrapping the entire development of certain games. In 1998, he was honored as the first inductee into the Academy of Interactive Arts and Sciences' Hall of Fame, was chosen as one of *TIME Magazine's* 100 Most Influential People of the Year in 2007 and 2008, and on March 7, 2007, received the Lifetime Achievement Award at the Game Developers Choice Awards.

Nintendo

Originally headquartered in Kyoto, Japan, but now with offices spanning the globe, Nintendo has clearly surpassed its humble beginnings in 1889 as a playing card company. According to a company press release, as of October 2, 2008, Nintendo had sold more than 470 million hardware units and 2.7 billion software units. The earnings release for fiscal year ending March 31, 2009, reported that the company's net income was ¥279.089 and it employed 4,130 people.

In 1974, Nintendo secured the rights to distribute the Magnavox Odyssey home video game console in Japan. Three years later, the company introduced the Color TV Game home video game console. Four versions of these consoles were produced, each playing variations on a single game (for example, Color TV Game 6 featured six versions of *Light Tennis*). During this same time, Shigeru Miyamoto was hired by Nintendo and went on to create some of Nintendo's most famous video games—most notably *Mario Bros.* and *Donkey Kong*—and became one of the most recognizable faces in the video game industry. Nintendo has since gone on to secure its place in the annals of video game history, with solidly popular gaming systems like the Game Boy and the Wii.

PopCap Games

This casual game developer and publisher, based in Seattle, Washington, was founded in 2000 by John Vechey, Brian Fiete, and Jason Kapalka, and currently employs more than 180 people. Most of PopCap's games can be played free in a limited form, with the full version available for a fee. The company's flagship title *Bejeweled* has sold more than 25 million units across all major platforms and was inducted into the Computer Gaming World Hall of Fame in 2002. Part of the company's success is based on the fact that its games can be played on a wide variety of platforms: Web, PC and Mac, Xbox, Xbox 360, PlayStation 3, cell phones, PDAs, iPhones, and other mobile devices.

Sony

Sony Corporation, headquartered in Minato, Tokyo, Japan, is one of the leading manufacturers of electronics, video, communications, video game consoles, and information technology products for the consumer and professional markets. Sony Online Entertainment (SOE), headquartered in San Diego, California, is the game development and game publishing division of Sony and is best known for creating massively multiplayer online games (MMORPG), including *EverQuest*, *EverQuest II, PlanetSide, Star Wars Galaxies, Free Realms,* and *Vanguard:*

Saga of Heroes. The company has additional game development studios in Austin, Texas; Denver, Colorado; and Seattle, Washington.

Where Will Video Games Go in the Future?

Obviously, as technology in general improves and advances, and as new innovations in computing are put forth, video games will also evolve, with new aspects of game play and new ways to immerse players in the game, perhaps. However, the future of video games potentially goes beyond the games themselves to other, perhaps more practical applications.

Military Uses

For years, the U.S. armed forces have used big, sophisticated simulators with hydraulics systems, giant video screens, and realistic cockpits. But this equipment costs millions of dollars and thus is not widely available. The solution? Video games. Acknowledging the fact that most recruits today grew up playing video games, the Pentagon and the Army have been using such simulations to train and recruit soldiers. Even the Central Intelligence Agency is developing a role-playing computer simulation to train analysts. Simulation games such as *Full Spectrum Warrior* and *Full Spectrum Command* help recruits and trainees go beyond the shoot 'em up video game and learn how to lead. *Full Spectrum Command* involves light infantry company commanders who lead about 120 people. Set in Eastern Europe, it tests organization, decision making, and the ability to recognize threats in a peacekeeping setting. With *Full Spectrum Warrior*, squad leaders command nine soldiers in complex, confusing urban-warfare scenarios. The game currently under development with the CIA puts agency analysts in the role of terror-cell leaders, cell members, and operatives. "Our analysts would be accustomed to looking at the world from the perspective of the terrorists we are chasing, and learn to expect the unexpected," said CIA spokesman Mark Mansfield.

Retail versions of the games currently used by the Army and Army National Guard for training are under development and expected to be released within the next few years. However, there is no plan to release a public version of the CIA's simulation. In the meantime, there's always the video game version of *24*.

Medical Uses

It should be no surprise that medical schools and other facilities have been making use of simulations for quite some time now. Granted, inserting a catheter in a video game is not quite the same as doing it in real life; however, it does help students and trainees get a feel for the procedure. But the medical use of video games is going beyond the basic simulation of common practices and procedures, and delving into aspects previously unimagined.

For example, at the American Geriatrics Society's 2007 Annual Scientific Meeting, a 3-D virtual reality video game called *RiskDom-Geriatrics* was unveiled. The game, designed to train medical students to make effective home visits, simulated a patient's home, and, among other things, allowed players to explore and evaluate the home for hazards that could lead to falls and other injuries. According to an article in *Medical News Today*, "preliminary data found that medical students who were evaluated before and after playing and had to play against time and distractions, showed improvements in their understanding of how to make an effective home visit." Home visits are a vital aspect in the care of elderly people so these findings mean that health professionals who make home visits can do so more effectively and more efficiently after spending time with this game.

Video games are also being used to help aid stroke patients in the recovery process. In a small study, 10 stroke victims (with an average age of 57) played virtual reality games in which they imagined they were diving with sharks or snowboarding down a narrow slope. As a result, their ability to walk eventually improved. While this study was admittedly small, the findings are promising, especially when viewed in light of the fact that participants had experienced their strokes more than a year before the study took place and were not expected to recover further.

Then there are games like *Ben's Game*, which resulted when eight-year-old Ben Duskin, a leukemia patient, contacted game programmer Eric Johnson through the Make-a-Wish Foundation. Duskin credited video game play with his ability to cope with his disease and its treatment, and he wanted to create something that could help other kids in similar situations. In the game, the player skates around a stylized field of cells on a rocket-powered surfboard and battles monsters representing the side effects of chemotherapy. While the game may not exactly advance medical knowledge, it is significant for other reasons—by creating games that help distract

INTERVIEW

You Need More Than Just a Love of Games

Todd MacIntyre
Senior Producer, Big Blue Bubble

How long have you been in this industry? What was your introduction to it?
Thirteen years. I started in the industry as a beta tester for a game developer. A friend got me the job, which I thought was only going to be a temporary position until I found a permanent career position; however, I just never left the industry.

What are the hot areas in the video game industry? Have you seen them change over time or have they remained relatively the same?
The hot areas in the games industry has always been how to get players more integrated into the games so they become more and more immersed in them. This "overall" area hasn't changed, but the means at which companies are getting players immersed has changed due to the changing technologies (i.e., the Wii motion controls and the iPhone/iPod touch), the cultural trends (i.e., social networking like Facebook and MySpace), and improved Internet/network technology.

What trends have you noticed as far as job opportunities? Can you predict any new trends? What developments took you by surprise?
Job opportunities were quite available until we hit the recession in late 2008. After that, jobs were scarce and difficult to secure due to the sheer number of people that had been laid off from large companies like Sony, Microsoft, and EA. This created a lot of competition for people who wanted to stay in the industry and were contending for jobs in an industry that not only saw a loss of jobs because of company layoffs, but also saw companies close down completely. Fortunately, the gaming industry is one that does not feel the effects of recessions as much as many other industries so the prospects do seem to be improving faster than other industries.

New trends in gaming seem to be more and more companies [recognizing] the value of having writers on staff. Games have production values that rival the movie industry, and game developers are seeing that having a good narrative is beginning to be just as important as great graphics and realistic physics. We are still early in this trend, and I think we still have a while to go before a video game writer becomes a common appearance in game industry job ads. It is common in the large companies because they have the larger development budgets, but it will be a while before developers feel writers are a necessity to have on staff.

The one development that took me by surprise and is still surprising me to this day is how undervalued game designers are. There is too much of a hierarchy in companies right now where the programmer is the king of the hill, with artists approaching the crest of the hill and designers still being at the bottom of the hill. You can make amazing physics, AI, and awesome graphics, but that does not make a killer game. It will attract people's attention (like a movie with lots of explosions), but if the game does not pull the player in with good controls, rewarding layouts, enjoyable interactions, cool power-ups, and items then players will not play the game to the end. Instead, they will get frustrated and bored (after the excitement of the explosions and rag-doll physics wears off) and go to another game. I thought by now developers would have seen the advantages of good design and designers would be benefiting from the demand of their skills, but this still hasn't been realized through the industry (with the exception of a handful of well known people like Miyamoto and Bleszinski), and the designers are still the runts of the groups that get pushed around and too often code or art dictates design instead of design dictating what needs to be done in code or what art assets need to be done.

What strengths/talents do you think make someone well suited for the video game industry?

Adaptability: There are so many types of games out there that people need to be able to work on games of any genre (including games targeting little kids). You do not always get to work on your dream game—or even the genre you like to play the most—so you need to be able to work on different games and still be able to get enjoyment from doing your job.

Focus: Things change frequently while developing a game, so people need to be able to change gears easily to redirect their attention and focus on the new destination or targets. Something as simple as the game engine not being able to handle something will require a person to have to look at assets in a different way, thus they need to be able to look at things in a different way often.

(continues on next page)

INTERVIEW

You Need More Than Just a Love of Games (continued)

Objective: You cannot go into game development with the "fan-boy" attitude. Thinking that a game [has lots] of merit is one thing, but thinking it is the best game ever and nothing can compare it is having too much tunnel vision. Games borrow and influence each other across all genres, and you cannot just focus on one game or even one genre to be successful. You need to be able to see the qualities of virtually every game out there and be able to tell what virtues of the game are good are bad even if you do not play the genre. Being open-minded to every-thing out there will give you that advantage over developers who only look at what other games in the same genre they are developing for.

While there is no formal "career plan" per se, how does one go about planning a career in video games? How valuable is a mentor in this field?
The best way to plan a career path in the games industry is to talk to as many people in the profession as possible and ask a lot of questions. The games industry does not have as many inaccessible people as many other industries have (i.e., movie industry), and many are more than willing to answer questions (provided they have the time). So sending a few e-mails to companies will usually have a chance of getting a response from "someone." It might not always be the person you want to hear from, but you will get someone's perspective on get-ting into games and how they broke into the industry.

Another good way to get information about getting into game development is to attend game conferences that are occurring all over

children who are in constant pain, these young patients may just gain the edge they need to fight and overcome leukemia and other devastating illnesses.

Video Games in the Classroom

While the idea may not thrill parents who already think their chil-dren spend too much time playing video games, the fact remains that video games can be an effective educational tool and can be applied to fields as wide-ranging as history, physics, and geography.

the world. There are also many local events that can get you in touch with smaller companies who can give you lots of information on how the games industry operates because they have had to build their small company from nothing and have great stories of the experiences they had to overcome.

Also, get in on the ground floor of a new company and, if you are able to financially, volunteer there. This will give you some insight on the inner workings of the studio and let you know if this is something you think you can handle or not.

Having a mentor will give [you a good idea] of what happens on a day-to-day basis in a studio, and you will see many things happen and crises will pop up that have to be dealt with that might not normally be seen. Witnessing these surprises and how they get handled would be an incredible opportunity for anyone.

What is the most important thing someone needs to know who is considering entering the video game industry today?
Just because you can play games really well and you dominate anyone you play against does not make you a good video game developer. Many think that just because they love games and can beat every game they play that they will be great at creating games. This is not necessarily true. For example, just because you can read fast does not mean you would be a great writer. There is a lot more to gaming than just being able to play them well, and many are surprised that they do not actually play the game as much as they would think when they are making it. Usually you are just testing out the function or art that you just worked on instead of running through the entire level or world. You just do not have the time to do that sort of thing because you have to make the fixes you need, get the items implemented, and move onto the next task.

To that end, Kurt Squire, associate professor of education at the University of Wisconsin at Madison, and James Paul Gee, a UW-Madison curriculum and instruction professor, were tapped to serve as instructors for a workshop on video gaming and literacy. Squire and colleagues at MIT created a game called *Supercharged!* that had players navigate through magnetically charged mazes. In order to be successful at the game, players had to understand how atomic particles worked. According to Squire, students at a middle school in Waltham, Massachusetts, who played the game "outperformed those who used a traditional curriculum by 20 percent in a final test of main concepts." Another game, called *Revolution*, uses Colonial Williamsburg to teach history.

An offshoot of this workshop, the Education Arcade, is an initiative that hopes to raise teacher awareness of the effectiveness of game-playing in education, encourage software developers to come up with new educational games, and build markets for their products.

Will the Wii Revolutionize Game Play?

When the Wii was first under development, Nintendo's plan was originally to call the console "Revolution." However, video game consoles are typically abbreviated—both for ease of use and perhaps because it happens anyhow among users. There was no clever way to shorten Revolution, so Nintendo changed tack—much to everyone's amusement and derision at first. The company chose the name Wii to emphasize the console's all-inclusive nature and design. The console is designed for everyone rather than just a select group of hardcore gamers. Rather than trying to take on the big boys and their big toys (which Nintendo had tried—and failed—to do with the GameCube), this time the company was deliberately unobtrusive and quiet. The console is small and white and rather nondescript. It is not as powerful as the PlayStation or Xbox, but it succeeded fantastically at drawing people to it who were otherwise uninterested, if not slightly intimidated by, video games. With a price half of that of the PlayStation, the Wii experienced success that no one ever imagined. In fact, according to Kate Berens and Geoff Howard, authors of *The Rough Guide to Videogames*, "the Wii's components weren't being manufactured quickly enough to supply the astonishing level of demand for the console." The release of Wii-Fit, with its pressure-sensitive balance board saw the console being accepted by an even wider segment of the population. Whether all these Wii players will in turn become players of other games and game systems remains to be seen. What is undeniable is that the Wii has changed not only how video games are played, but how they are marketed.

What About Second Life?

Second Life is a virtual world developed by Linden Lab that launched in 2003. Essentially a community of people connected via the Internet, *Second Life* allows users to socialize with one another, trade goods and services, and travel to each other's countries, all by acting through their virtual personas, or avatars. The original *Second Life* program is intended for adults over age 18, while a newer version called *Teen Second Life* is targeted at youths between 13 and 17.

The question in the industry, however, is whether or not *Second Life* is truly a video game. Given the definition used throughout this book, not really. There are no quests, there are no goals, there is no growth of the character per se, there is not even a backstory beyond what each player brings to the game and creates for his or her avatar. Spend just a little bit of time in *Second Life* and you will be amazed at the depth and breadth of its applications: commerce, education, religion, sports, gaming, recreation, "adult entertainment"—even countries like the Maldives, Sweden, Estonia, and Colombia have established embassies on this virtual world. *Second Life* is not a video game, yet it perhaps shows us the future of video games. As technology evolves, as video games—regardless of the platform on which they are played—become more complex, players are drawn into the game, becoming the characters they know better than they know themselves. Consoles like Nintendo's Wii and Microsoft's Project Natal respond to the players' actual movements to direct game play. From there, it is literally a hop, skip, and a jump to interacting in a virtual world, forsaking the real one. Whether this will be a boon or a bane remains to be seen.

Video Games and Addiction: Is It Really Possible?

While there are undoubtedly people throughout the world who would claim vociferously that their children, significant other, spouse, or even themselves are addicted to video games, is it a true addiction? The answer is yes—and for the same reason that addictions to alcohol, gambling, or drugs are true addictions. While the mainstream medical community is not quite ready to acknowledge video game addiction on the same level as addiction to alcohol (or even compulsive gambling, for that matter), the fact is that games are designed to suck players in to the exclusion of all else. "That is the main goal you have when you design a game," says Jason Kapalka, co-founder of casual game company PopCap. PopCap's business model, like that of most casual game companies, is "try before you buy." So it is important to grab players quickly so that they will actually purchase the game. The stunning popularity of their games *Peggle* and *Bejeweled* are a testament to this model's success. But this does not mean that

INTERVIEW

A Combination of Passion and Determination

Losmanto
2-D/Texture Artist, Matahari Studios

How long have you been in this industry? What was your introduction/what drew you to it?
I've worked in this field for five years. I could say it was passion that drove me to this industry. I've been a gamer and comic fan since I was eight years old. Since then, I was always fascinated by art and illustrations and how those games were made.

What are the hot areas in the video game industry? Have they changed over time or remained the same?
I think the hot areas would be the art and technology. I cannot say the same thing about game design because almost every game I've played until now [has only changed slightly with regard to game play]. On the other hand, the technology [and ways in which art is created is growing] rapidly. Players are [becoming] more demanding and choosier, so the industry must not remain creatively stagnant whether it is in art or technology.

What trends have you noticed as far as job opportunities? Can you predict any new trends?
The trend currently has to do with technology. Competition with regard to next-gen consoles, for example, pushes progress in game

designers are deliberately trying to make games "addictive" per se—what they are trying to do is create games that are compelling and thus, successful.

Perhaps it is not the game play itself that is so addictive, but rather the interaction with the community, the social network that springs up around games like *Halo* and *World of Warcraft*. According to Clint Worley, senior producer on Sony's *EverQuest*, "The social networking is really kind of the glue that pushes people to sit in the game for long periods of time." Dr. Hilarie Cash, a therapist in Redmond, Washington, who specializes in Internet and computer addiction, agrees. She works with teenagers and young men in their 20s who do not have a lot going on in the real world so they play online games to fill the development. The recent breakthrough technologies are Project Natal and 4-D experience. I believe the new trends would be more realistic graphics and virtual technology.

What strengths and talents do you think make someone well suited for the video game industry?
A person who can boost their own creativity, is eager to learn new things, is competitive, a dreamer, passionate, disciplined, and can work as a team player is capable of doing anything in the video game industry.

How does one go about planning a career in video games? How valuable is a mentor in this field?
It is all about passion and how far you [will] go to achieve your dreams. Gamers and artists usually are dreamers—a career in video games is considered a dream come true to those who love to do their hobbies while making money from them. Mentors are more valuables than books, tutorials, and trainings because they [bring you up to speed much faster than anything else].

What do you consider the biggest myth about the video game industry, if any?
[While working in this field may be a "dream come true," do not think] you can make your own creation and [the gaming world will instantly recognize] how good you are. The fact is you must always rely on the demands of many people—clients, producers, art directors, and developers, among others—however, this can also boost your skill set and you will always learn something new.

void of friendship, companionship—even love. "What I see in the population that I'm working with ...many gamers are people who were bored and lonely, and this is an addiction which kind of gets its hooks into them," she says.

So what is a video game addict to do? The answer is the same as with any addiction: Acknowledge the problem and then take steps to overcome it. In some cases, this may require professional help. In other cases, it may involve taking a step back, taking a deep breath, and jumping back into the real world. Not surprisingly, gamers can be an out-of-shape group. Replacing a few hours a week of game play with a few hours at the gym may be all it takes to regain balance and perspective again in one's life. After all, it is just a game!

Video Games and Violence: Myth or Reality?

The answer is actually a blend between the two, depending on your perspective. Granted, some games are just in outright poor taste and one wonders why anyone in development ever thought the concept was a good idea—consider games such as *JKF: Reloaded, Postal*, and *Custer's Revenge* for examples of games that just leave the general public shaking their head in bafflement. (Thankfully, these games were short-lived.) However, there is absolutely no evidence to date linking acts of violence with video game play—despite what activist groups might otherwise believe. In fact, authors Kate Berens and Geoff Howard report that "since *Doom* put 3-D shooters into the mainstream, violent crime has actually dropped, according to the U.S. Department of Justice." Other research supports this finding. Clearly, as authors Berens and Howard go on to state, "the fraction of the population who both play video games and have also committed heinous crimes may simply represent that percentage of natural born killers already in our midst."

One of the earliest and best-known games in the center of this debate is *Mortal Kombat*. Originally developed by Midway, the game involved martial arts-style combat between fighters of varying strengths and talents. What got the moral majority up in arms were the gory ways in which players could finish off one another—by ripping off an opponent's head, for example, with the spine still attached. The Nintendo version was tamed down a bit—sweat droplets replaced most of the droplets of blood—and the game's lack of popularity was a direct result of such tweaking. In 1993, congressional hearings were held to address the issue of violence in video games, the outcome of which was the adoption of an industry-wide ratings system that is still in existence today. Known as the Entertainment Software Ratings Board (ESRB), the system is "designed to provide concise and impartial information about the content in computer and video games so consumers, especially parents, can make an informed purchase decision." Rating symbols suggest age appropriateness for the game, and content descriptors indicate elements in a game that may have triggered a particular rating or may be of interest or concern. The ratings are as follows:

Early Childhood: Titles rated EC have content that may be suitable for ages 3 and older. Contains no material that parents would find inappropriate.

Everyone: Titles rated E have content that may be suitable for ages 6 and older. Titles in this category may contain minimal cartoon, fantasy, or mild violence and/or infrequent use of mild language.

Everyone 10+: Titles rated E10+ have content that may be suitable for ages 10 and older. Titles in this category may contain more cartoon, fantasy or mild violence, mild language, and/or minimal suggestive themes.

Teen: Titles rated T have content that may be suitable for ages 13 and older. Titles in this category may contain violence, suggestive themes, crude humor, minimal blood, simulated gambling, and/or infrequent use of strong language.

Mature: Titles rated M have content that may be suitable for persons ages 17 and older. Titles in this category may contain intense violence, blood and gore, sexual content, and/or strong language.

Adults Only: Titles rated AO have content that should only be played by persons 18 years and older. Titles in this category may include prolonged scenes of intense violence and/or graphic sexual content and nudity.

Rating Pending: Titles listed as RP have been submitted to the ESRB and are awaiting final rating. (This symbol appears only in advertising prior to a game's release.)

ESRB content descriptors are as follows:

Alcohol Reference: Reference to and/or images of alcoholic beverages

Animated Blood: Discolored and/or unrealistic depictions of blood

Blood: Depictions of blood

Blood and Gore: Depictions of blood or the mutilation of body parts

Cartoon Violence: Violent actions involving cartoon-like situations and characters. May include violence where a character is unharmed after the action has been inflicted

Comic Mischief: Depictions or dialogue involving slapstick or suggestive humor

Crude Humor: Depictions or dialogue involving vulgar antics, including "bathroom" humor

Drug Reference: Reference to and/or images of illegal drugs

Fantasy Violence: Violent actions of a fantasy nature, involving human or non-human characters in situations easily distinguishable from real life

Intense Violence: Graphic and realistic-looking depictions of physical conflict. May involve extreme and/or realistic blood, gore, weapons, and depictions of human injury and death

Language: Mild to moderate use of profanity

Lyrics: Mild references to profanity, sexuality, violence, alcohol, or drug use in music

Mature Humor: Depictions or dialogue involving "adult" humor, including sexual references

Nudity: Graphic or prolonged depictions of nudity

Partial Nudity: Brief and/or mild depictions of nudity

Real Gambling: Player can gamble, including betting or wagering real cash or currency

Sexual Content: Non-explicit depictions of sexual behavior, possibly including partial nudity

Sexual Themes: References to sex or sexuality

Sexual Violence: Depictions of rape or other violent sexual acts

Simulated Gambling: Player can gamble without betting or wagering real cash or currency

Strong Language: Explicit and/or frequent use of profanity

Strong Lyrics: Explicit and/or frequent references to profanity, sex, violence, alcohol, or drug use in music

Strong Sexual Content: Explicit and/or frequent depictions of sexual behavior, possibly including nudity

Suggestive Themes: Mild provocative references or materials

Tobacco Reference: Reference to and/or images of tobacco products

Use of Drugs: The consumption or use of illegal drugs

Use of Alcohol: The consumption of alcoholic beverages

Use of Tobacco: The consumption of tobacco products

Violence: Scenes involving aggressive conflict; may contain bloodless dismemberment

Violent References: References to violent acts

The next few chapters will delve into the nuts and bolts of the industry, with a look at the many different jobs that go into bringing a video game to life and what they entail, ways to advance your career (and things that can forestall it), and terms and jargon you need to know as a video game professional.

Chapter 3

On the Job

When launching a career in the video game industry, it helps to understand the duties and responsibilities of people in key positions. Also, some career paths in this industry are more natural than others. For example, a designer may be more likely to move into production work, or a programmer may be more likely to move into animation.

This chapter discusses the key positions in the video game industry. Positions are listed alphabetically within the following categories: Where possible, opportunities for career advancement are mentioned and connections among positions are provided. In addition, related positions are listed so that areas of crossover may be more readily identified. Additional information can be found in chapter 6 and, for some positions, in the U.S. Bureau of Labor Statistics' *Occupational Outlook Handbook* (2008–2009) (the handbook does not have information for all positions discussed in this chapter).

Design

Game design is what many people think of when they consider a career in the video game industry. Often viewed as "sexy" and glamorous, design involves coming up with the idea for a game; defining how it is going to work as a system of rules (remember, when all is said and done, a game is just a piece of software and, as such, must operate according to rules); describing the elements and features that constitute it; and communicating this information to all the other members of the team. Design is perhaps the most collaborative position in this industry—often, the game you initially envisioned is not reflected in the final product because everyone has ideas and suggestions (some better—or more feasible—than others). The design team is often the most involved at the beginning of a project, and the most successful game designers possess the following skills and qualities:

➡ **Imagination:** This is not just coming up with a great idea. People are imaginative in different ways. Some people can come up with strong, detailed characters and fantastic plots; others are better at envisioning how the game will work as a whole. And some people are especially skilled in what is called lateral thinking—the ability to take what is familiar and put an unexpected twist on it. This is perhaps one of the most important qualities a designer needs to have.

➡ **Writing:** This does not mean writing dialog or scripts or even user interface text. There are actual writers who handle these and other tasks. However, designers have to document several aspects of game design—the ideas, how they will be brought to fruition, what team members are responsible for, what decisions have been made and what decisions still need to be made, and more. In order to communicate these things clearly and effectively, a successful designer knows the rules of grammar and spelling, and knows how to put a sentence together.

➡ **Technical skills:** As with writing, designers do not necessarily have to be programmers (although some have been and then moved into design), but they do need to understand what the software they use can and cannot do. As has been emphasized elsewhere in this book, it is knowing what software cannot do that is perhaps the more important technical skill. If you come up with a design that the current software just cannot support, you've wasted time and money—commodities that are often in short supply.

➡ **Analytical skills:** As mentioned, a game is a system with a set of rules, and the successful game designer knows how to approach the design of a game in an analytical fashion. This is all about cause and effect. How are the relationships between things like hit points, strength, life, and armor going to be expressed? Where is the balance between the action a character carries out and the effect it has on the game's world? In order to see these and other relationships and translate them into game play, you must possess an analytical, logical mind. This also helps you to create a game that fits nicely within the constraints of software, time, money, and resources.

➡ **Math skills:** Along with an ability to analyze the rules of the game and how play is going to be carried out, designers need to basic understanding of math. For example, you have a group of 200 soldiers and 100 yards away is a group of 500 orcs. If the soldiers start shooting at 100 yards, how many orcs will still be alive by the time they reach the soldiers? (And you thought you had escaped story problems...) Granted, there are probably tools out there that can help with these tasks, but if you want to work on intricate, complex games you need to understand how to solve problems such as these. This goes hand in hand with knowing what is possible in a game and what is not, and helps give the game a realistic feel.

➡ **A sense of aesthetics:** This is where designers and artists collaborate to bring to life the characters and the world the designer has envisioned. Again, the designer is not expected to be an artist, but she is expected to have a sense of taste and style. This is where imagination comes into play. As author Ernest Adams states, "Lazy designers copy what other games do; good designers create worlds with a fresh new look that impresses everyone."

➡ **Research skills:** So if you are working on a fantasy game, pretty much anything goes when it comes to what a troll looks like, for example, and what kind of damage it can do. However, designers who work on games such as *Tom Clancy's Rainbow Six*, *Medal of Honor*, or even *Grand Theft Auto* need to know as much as possible about ammunition, special ops, cars, and more. A flight simulation game is going to want designers on their team who are actual pilots. These people will know the point at which a given aircraft will stall, for example, and will know what maneuvers a particular aircraft can do and which ones it cannot. However, when people with specialized knowledge are not on a team, the successful designer knows how to quickly research—both online and in a library—and uncover the information he or she needs to make that game as realistic as possible.

Assistant Designer

This is the point where a designer typically begins his or her career. The scope of responsibility is small—an assistant designer often works on just one aspect of a game, such as designing a weapon for a barbarian or the instrument panel of a plane. The assistant designer also may be responsible for updating and maintaining the design document. The design document is a vital component and serves as the blueprint for the game. It explains—in excruciating detail—all aspects of the game's design. This can be a daunting task for the assistant designer, especially since this document can be neglected

On the Cutting
Edge

Think that 3-D is as far as video game technology can go? Think again. Research and development is currently underway on 4-D technology. In general, 4-D refers to a coordinate system composed of four axes, all at right angles from each other. Three of these coordinates are in space; the fourth is a position in time, where time is considered mathematically as a fourth axis that is at right angles to the other axes. Thus, with respect to video game play, this would involve length, width, height, and depth. Whether this technology is even possible—or could truly be captured as 4-D and not just another aspect of 3-D sparks fierce debate among the video game community. Some argue that the games would be so hard to navigate in as to be nearly impossible. Others argue that if you provide players with 3-D glasses, any limitations could be overcome (the dilemma is in trying to create a realistic 4-D game in a 2-D environment—the monitor or screen). Perhaps as technology in general advances the possibilities of 4-D will become clearer.

as development on the game progresses. Nonetheless, the design document can play a vital role when it comes to testing the game, so it is best to put in the effort and keep it as current as possible.

Associate Designer

Assistant designers typically become associate designers. These people work closely with the lead designers, taking on whatever responsibilities and tasks the lead designer cannot get to. The scope of responsibility of an associate designer is bigger than you might think, often involving a huge chunk of the actual game. These are people that have proven that they can go beyond what is expected of an assistant designer—and probably are capable of becoming a lead designer—they just are not quite there. Yet.

Editor

Editors are responsible for ensuring the accuracy of the writing. This may include basic copyediting skills, like checking grammar, spelling, and punctuation, but also can include ensuring that the material the writer has produced is well organized, easy to understand, accurate, and thorough. Most of the time, editors work closely with writers, but they can also work with developers, programmers, and project managers. They also work with the graphics or production departments to make sure that screen images and art are laid out properly. As with writers, editors often work in the video game field in a freelance capacity, which is often the case with video game publishers; or they may work for a publications department in a specific company. Related fields include technical writing, multimedia development, Web site design, and project management.

Game Designer

This position is a step above a level designer, but the responsibilities are quite different. Whereas a level designer is concerned just with one mission, for example, the game designer takes the overall concept of the game and brings it to life, deciding how the goals of the game will be carried out based on the core mechanics of the game (the rules of this game system, in other words). Where is the game located and what does this world look like? What characters live in this world? How do they look and how do they behave? The game designer answers all these questions and more. He or she defines the rules by which the player will fulfill the game's mission—this includes all the sights and sounds, although it is the job of the art and audio departments to actually create those things. For example, in a game like *Peggle*, it is the game designer who decided that the "board" would be a design of blue and orange pegs arranged in various patterns, with a "launcher" that sends a ball into play, which lights up pegs it hits while it falls to the bottom of the screen. Green pegs give the player certain powers, depending on the character a player is utilizing.

This is not an entry-level position, although this does not mean that an especially strong candidate with an exceptional portfolio cannot land a job as a game designer. The usual track, however, is to start at the assistant level (perhaps at the associate level) and then become a level designer and work into a game designer job from there. The salary ranges from $40,000 to $75,000, depending on experience.

Keeping in Touch

It is important for your career that you join community forums, online competitions, or collaborative production. This will help ensure that your skills keep pace with industry standards and broaden your network of connections in the industry. Get your work recognized in online forum communities. This will quickly establish your reputation—however, make sure to acknowledge and respect the work of others as well.

Lead Designer

The lead designer is responsible for the game's design in its entirety. He or she understands the overall creative vision of the game and will ensure that this vision is adhered to until the end, from the big picture to the tiniest detail. The lead designer manages the other designers, categorizing the game design into chunks and handing them off to the other team members for development. Going back to the *Peggle* example, if the game designer is the person who envisions what game play will look like and how it will be carried out, it is the lead designer who knows that the game is designed to be a variation of the arcade pinball games, translated into virtual form and using different-colored pegs to represent different points and features; and the object of the game is to hit all the orange pegs on the board in 10 moves or less.

This is definitely not an entry-level position, no matter how impressive your portfolio or previous work experience may be. You must work in a company for several years in order to earn a promotion to this spot. The salary range is from $75,000 to $100,000, depending on experience.

Level Designer

The level designer is responsible for just one level or mission of the game. They decide what a player's goal is at a particular moment in the game. Level designers take the elements and mechanics of the game and use a level editor to create the challenges and obstacles that the player will face. A level editor—also known as a map, campaign, or scenario editor—is a software application used to design (what else?) levels, maps, or campaigns for a game. (Sometimes, a level editor is integrated into the game; its features will sometimes be disabled in the version of the software that is released to market; more often, however, it is a separate application).

As author Ernest Adams notes, "Although level designers have the least amount of design authority over the interior mechanics of the game, they have the greatest effect on the player's actual experience of it." Level designers often work with testers and other designers to ensure that the game works as designed and that there is balance— for example, if the same strategy always causes the player to win or if there is a certain feature that really no longer has a purpose now that it is implemented into the game, it is the level designer who notes this and brings it to the attention of the appropriate person.

This can be an entry-level position, especially since many games come with a level editor. With a game that has a level editor built in, you can create your own levels and build a portfolio.

Writer

While designers typically write game content, writers can be brought in to create a wide range of materials in support of video games: books, manuals, documents, online help systems, tutorials, reference books, Web site text, and more. They are also responsible for writing text that appears within a user interface—tooltips, for example, or the text that appears in pop-up messages or dialog boxes. When working on a game in the *Star Wars* franchise, for example, outside writers are utilized more heavily. The authors of *Game Plan* point out that "in this case, the writer works closely with the director and lead game designer to craft a coherent context for game play. The writer is concerned with ...story structure, setting, dialogue, character development, setups and payoffs, plot twists, and pacing." Writers often have to work with the development team and programmers, staying in the loop about how a game is supposed to work, what its features are, how they can best meet users' needs, and so on. Technical writers who work on a freelance basis can take their career in nearly any direction they choose, provided they are motivated and self-disciplined enough. These are not typically full-time positions. Instead, writers are often brought in on a freelance basis to work on a particular game only. Related fields include technical editing, Web site design, and graphics.

Production

While everyone involved in a video game is responsible for making sure that things stay on track and on schedule, the production team is specifically concerned with this aspect. It is the production team's responsibility to ensure that the video game is delivered on time and within the assigned budget—and to scramble like crazy when things pop up that affect these two very important things! As you might expect, sometimes there can be friction between the design team, who wants a little more time to fine-tune a feature, and the production team, who thinks the game is just fine as it is, thank you, and wants to move it out the door on time. The team lead then steps in and mediates a solution that makes everyone happy. While some video game developers have a production team in-house, in many cases, the production team works on behalf of the publisher.

Producers can be responsible for more than one game at a time, and, depending on their level in the company hierarchy, may be overseeing a few production areas or the entire production process. Producers are the generalists of the video game world—they have to know about all aspects of a game's development. While a producer may not be expected to step in and write code, create a 3-D animation model, or compose a soundtrack, he or she is expected to have at least a rudimentary understanding of the tasks and tools involved in video game design. The really great ones can step in and help out in a pinch. In addition, the producer often has the last word regarding any creative decisions that need to be made, but this does not mean that he or she has sole authority. Producers generally work with designers in these sorts of cases.

Specific responsibilities of a producer can include such things as:

➡ Listen to game pitches from development companies

➡ Determine the size and scope of a project, including the budget, schedule, and who's going to do what

➡ Work with the lead game designer to develop the broad concept of the game

➡ Verify milestones during the course of the project

➡ Negotiate contracts with outside suppliers and vendors

➡ Act as a liaison between marketing, PR, legal, and other nontechnical departments

While not a position that requires the same sorts of specific skills that, say, a programmer, graphic artist, or animator must possess, producers are expected to have excellent project management, budgeting, and scheduling skills. "Softer skills" include:

➡ **Product sense:** This is the ability to tell if a game will be fun and will do well commercially. What is more, it is also the ability to tell how to tweak a not-so-popular game so that it becomes successful. This is not necessarily something a person either has or does not have. While some people just naturally have a better product sense than others, product sense can be honed by playing as many different games as possible (including games you are not normally interested in), having years of experience in the industry, and thoroughly understanding your target audience, among other things.

➡ **Leadership:** As with product sense, this is both a talent and a skill. Some people are natural-born leaders; others acquire leadership skills as they advance in their career. As author Ernest Adams points out, "A producer is a head of a team of people, and that means you have to lead: inspire, encourage, render judgment, and, when necessary, enforce discipline ...poor leadership has killed untold numbers of otherwise good game projects."

➜ **Communication skills:** While this one might seem obvious, as with many other positions in the video game industry, it is crucial that a producer have the ability to communicate effectively, both in oral and written forms.

➜ **Negotiation skills:** Producers often have to walk a fine line between making the publisher happy and keeping the developers satisfied. Negotiation is about finding a middle ground that everyone can live with (note this is not always the same thing as finding a solution that everyone is *happy* with). A person who is able to skillfully walk that fine line will find themselves moving up the production ladder in no time.

➜ **Organization skills:** Given all the myriad details that a producer at any level is tasked with overseeing, excellent organization skills are a must. Today's video games are behemoth projects, with at times hundreds of people working on them and thousands of tasks. The producer has to know what is going on with a video game at any point in the development schedule, even when an aspect of a video game's development is being outsourced.

➜ **Attention to detail**: This goes hand in hand with organization. Because producers are responsible for so many things, the successful ones have an eye for the tiniest details. This does not mean micromanaging and handling every single detail personally, however. Producers are also excellent delegators, and efficient ones know how to assign aspects of the production process to an associate producer, for example.

Asset Manager

An asset is a data file needed for a specific component of the video game, whether that be audio, video, animation, and so on. The asset manager is tasked with overseeing all the thousands and thousands of assets that comprise the typical video game. Depending on the company and the complexity of the project, sometimes a sole person is assigned the role of asset manager; more often, managing assets is yet another responsibility for everyone working on the team, whether they be an animator or a producer. Every single aspect of a video game—sound file, image file, 3-D mesh, polygon, you name it—

must be named, tagged, and catalogued, and then managed throughout the development and production cycles. Because of the nearly overwhelming nature of this task, successful asset managers make extensive use of database systems to help them with this job. The salary ranges from $30,000 to $50,000.

Assistant Producer

This is the lowest level of the production ladder. Some people move to the production area from testing or development. The assistant producer supports the associate producer and other producers as necessary. Possible duties include shipping and receiving documents,

Professional
Ethics

So you are working for a company that makes educational video games for children, but what you really want to do is create a first-person shooter game that sets the video game world ablaze and spawns a lucrative franchise deal and movie rights to boot. While it is understood that people in the video game industry often have personal projects they work on away from the office, be careful not to start thinking of this as a separate business or a second job. Known as moonlighting, this practice can get you in trouble if you are not careful. For one thing, you are supposed to be working on behalf of the company that hired you, not against them. In extreme cases, you could be sued for theft or industrial espionage; at the very least, you could find yourself out of a job and hard-pressed for decent references. Make sure that the project you are working on is not something that could infringe on your employer's business. In the example given here, this is not likely to be a problem, given the disparity between an educational game and a shooter game. However, this is a grey area open to interpretation. No one is saying that you cannot work on personal projects, and the company certainly is not trying to tell you what to do when away from the office. The point is to be discrete and maintain your professionalism and responsibilities to the company that hired you. Maybe you want to even pitch them your game idea. It could lead to much bigger and better things.

equipment, and CDs to developers; making backups of all project material; testing milestone deliveries; assisting with game testing; and assisting with level design, among other things.

Associate Producer

Despite the subordinate-sounding word *associate*, the associate producer has a critical role in the production team. As the producer's go-to person, the associate producer steps in and handles anything the producer is not able to tackle, especially when it comes to internal team-related issues. The authors of *Game Plan* state that "this team-level focus is extremely important because it frees the producer to deal with the more company-wide issues, such as platforms, deadlines, and financial goals, many of which influence the project in important ways.

A sampling of tasks the associate producer is responsible for include:

→ Assisting the producer in budgeting and scheduling
→ Tracking the development team's progress
→ Helping the producer to maintain project documentation
→ Overseeing assistant producers
→ Attending trade shows and conferences
→ Running focus tests

The salary ranges from $30,000 to $50,000.

Executive Producer

An executive producer typically oversees a line of products—the *Star Wars*, *Mario*, or *Call to Duty* franchises, for example. There is little creative involvement with the actual game at this position, although executive producers are expected to still keep in touch with the "real world," so to speak, by playing the games in the line and reporting any comments and feedback. This is definitely not an entry-level position. The only way to earn this title is to ship successful games. Sample duties of an executive producer include:

→ Maintaining connections with marketing, sales, PR, and legal departments

➡ Negotiating development contract and license agreements

➡ Creating the company's product plan

External Producer

Some games are produced in-house; others are produced externally. In the latter case, a publisher often assigns an external producer the task of acting as a liaison between the developer and the publisher. As with executive producers, external producers often work on several projects at once, typically in the same line or franchise. This can be an exciting position, albeit a demanding one. Because the external producer is ultimately working on behalf of the publisher, he or she can be seen by the developer as either an ally or a threat. Successful external producers know how to skillfully walk this fine line, offering solutions so that the developers can do their job to the best of their abilities yet the publisher is happy because the game is remaining within the budgetary and scheduling constraints.

Internal Producer

The internal producer, while in this case working for the developer, still has to act as a liaison between the publishing and developing worlds. The duties and responsibilities are the same as with the external producer. William Westwater, a producer at Monolith Studios, describes the job as follows: "The internal producer's ...responsibility ...includes getting the team and design leads unified behind a coherent design, analyzing the design to create exciting mini-goals, and working with the team leads to determine how to reach those goals."

Localization Manager

Localization is the process of configuring a game so that it can be sold in another country. This involves changing the text and language—and sometimes the code and graphics as well (from a vertical to horizontal orientation, for example)—to the language of the destination country (or countries). The localization manager is the production person in charge of this process (salaries range from $30,000 to $50,000). The biggest markets outside the United States for U.S.-produced games are France, Germany, and Italy, thus, these are the most common languages for localized titles. (While Japan is also a major consumer of video games, most are locally produced; it is rare for a U.S. title to be released there.) Localization can be more difficult than you might think, because it encompasses so many different things, from installers and menu selections, to game hints and even the code in which the game is written and the console it is played on. Then there is the fact that different countries have different rating systems. Germany, for instance, has stricter laws about the use of violence in video games than does the United States. Often, a separate version of a game has to be created just for sale in Germany.

Production Assistant

This is a great entry-level position for a person new to the video game industry. The production assistant is responsible for doing practically everything and anything that members on the production team need, whether it is purchasing supplies, fielding phone calls, or bringing in take-out. As a result, it is a position that could potentially expose you to many different members of the team beyond product, which could allow you to make all sorts of connections. While it may sound like a gopher position, it is actually a rather important one, and a successful production assistant is a valuable resource indeed.

Technical Director

Technical directors are often used when a video game is being developed externally. Because producers do not usually have the technical expertise to judge the quality of programming by themselves, the technical director steps in and checks the development team's code to make sure that it meets certain software engineering standards. This position is also known as a technical advisor or technical producer. Other responsibilities of a technical director include tracking down and solving particularly difficult bugs and other technical problems, obtaining coding resources and tools for the team, and examining the proposed technical design of a game to determine if it is worth the publisher's efforts.

This is an advisory position, not a managerial one, although the technical director will verify certain project milestones with respect to code and authorize whether work should continue to the next phase (and if payment should be disbursed!). This also is not an entry-level position. Successful candidates must demonstrate proven programming experience—in particular, games programming—have extensive technical knowledge, and have years of experience working with software development teams.

Programming

Programming is at the heart of any and all video games—in fact, you do not have a video game without it, and programming can be the difference between a game that is just okay to play and a game that retailers cannot get on the shelves fast enough. It is the code programmers write that ties everything together. And while programmers certainly possess analytic, logical minds and have strong math skills, these are also creative people. Granted, they may not be creative in the same way that a designer or an artist or a musician is creative, but it takes a special kind of creativity to take the concepts of a video game and figure out how these will be expressed using bits and bytes of code. However, programmers only spend part of their time writing this code. Because all other video game assets—animation, art, audio, text, video, and so on—are dependent on the software, in addition to writing, documenting, testing, and debugging code, programmers routinely meet with design, art, and audio teams to work out the details and figure out how to put what is on the drawing board, so to speak, in the game.

In addition, because game programming is such a diverse field, people often pick a certain area and specialize. One of the most common specializations—and the one most currently in demand—is graphics programming. And this area can be broken down into subspecialties: 3-D graphics, animation, and video compression and playback. Other programming specialties include simulation, user interface programming, scripting languages, network and server programming, and security. Depending on the specialty, programmers make anywhere from $40,000 to $75,000.

Artificial Intelligence Programmer

Artificial intelligence (AI) is broadly defined as the science of making computers behave as if they were humans—specific areas of research and development have focused on learning, reasoning, problem-solving, perception, and language-understanding. With respect to video games, the AI programmer is the person responsible for making nonplayer characters (NPCs) behave as if they are think-ing, breathing, living, intelligent creatures. (NPCs are controlled by the video game rather than by the player.) AI programmers are highly sought after, and while all games require AI programming, it is more critical to some games than to others. Shooter games and sports games, for example, require AI programmers to really push the envelope and show their stuff. In particular, an AI programmer is responsible for designing and implementing AI structures through the use of artificial intelligence engines, programming activities that fit within the primary structure of the game, and working with the lead programmer to integrate AI strategies into the technical design and overall structure of the game. People in this field can make any-where from $40,000 to $75,000.

Engine Programmer

Engine programmers are responsible for building the primary foun-dation upon which the rest of the game is built. Often, various aspects of this foundation are divvied up among other programmers. For example, one programmer may be responsible for creating explosion effects, another one may be responsible for optimizing frame rate (the rate at which a computer or other display system displays new frames on a screen, measured in frames per second), and another programmer may be responsible for integrating special moves in a game (for example, that special button combo that causes a player to spin, kick, and deliver an uppercut almost simultaneously). Engine programmers tend to be specialists, knowing all there is about a specific aspect of programming, such as 3-D, 2-D, audio, or artificial intelligence.

Lead Programmer

The importance of the lead programmer cannot be overstated. This person is absolutely critical to the success of the project. The lead programmer (as the name implies) is responsible for taking the helm and leading the technical implementation of the game's design. As the authors of *Game Plan* state, "This person knows games, plays games, and has the technical ability to actually build games." Spe-cific duties include supervising all technical aspects of the game, including engine and tools development and debugging and techni-cal support after the game is released; ensuring that all programmers understand the ultimate architecture and vision of the game; delegating programming tasks, and making sure that these tasks are carried out according to schedule; and ensuring that all code is properly integrated. Successful lead programmers cannot only take existing technologies and create a game from them—they can create a game from the ground up. The salary ranges from $75,000 to $120,000.

Programmer

The programmers are the people who actually create the game as the designers envisioned it. They are responsible for writing code that implements the logic behind the game. For example, if a player must earn so many points before rising to another level, it is the programmer's job to implement this logic. Other tasks include coding vital 3-D components; integrating 3-D characters and environments into the game engine; optimizing and compiling game states and game scripts; and implementing the game framework, tools, and installer.

Tester

The tester plays a crucial role in a game's development. Do not think a tester just sits around playing games all day, however. Well, okay, testers *do* sit around all day playing games; however, they are not playing the games to win them, like the average user would. Rather, the tester plays the game according to a strict set of guidelines in order to test specific features. Successful testers have a keen eye for detail, good communication skills (you have to accurately and concisely document what went wrong during game play, after all), a decent amount of gaming ability, and patience. Patience is a more important virtue than you might think. Author Ernest Adams calls it a "key virtue" in a tester. While testers do not need to have programming knowledge, it certainly does not hurt to understand how a particular piece of software works and all the things that can go wrong with it. Testing falls into the following categories:

➡ **Bug testing:** Looking for software errors such as crash bugs, places where the game does not do what it is supposed to, or aesthetic defects (an upside-down tree, for example)

➡ **Configuration testing:** Playing the game on various types of PCs, for example, to be sure it will work on different systems

➜ **Game play testing and tuning:** Making the sure the game play is enjoyable and balanced (in other words, it is challenging, but not overly so)

➜ **Quality assurance:** Checking the game one last time before it is released to market (see the "Nontechnical Jobs" section for more information).

Tools Programmer

The tools programmer is responsible for creating the tools that the development team uses to create the game, thus, this position works closely with developers and designers. This person often has an in-depth knowledge of various game engines and is skilled in user interface design. The authors of *Game Plan* avow that "a well-conceived tool cannot be overstated. A good tool can actually speed up the development process ...freeing up the programmers to focus on what they do best."

Art

While design and development are certainly integral parts of a video game project, in a way, the art is even more important—after all, given today's technology and graphics capabilities, fans of video games have come to expect literally works of art—games with graphics that are so realistic as to look like a movie, with gorgeous environments and stunning special effects. The art team works with the designers to bring the design on paper to life on the screen, with the programmers so that they may better understand how to incorporate the art into the game, and with the audio department, who must synchronize sound effects to the animations the artists create. The process used to create a piece of art is called the production pipeline, and it involves the following steps: initial concept, 3-D model, motion-capture, animation, texturing, and generating the final file for use by the program.

Obviously, the members of the art team have a talent for drawing—and not just using the traditional media, such as pencils, inks, pens, paints, clay, and so on; they also are skillful in the use of software programs, including 3-D tools (such as 3ds, Maya, and Light-Wave) and 2-D tools (such as Photoshop, Illustrator, and Graphics Suite). Other tools artists often used include scanners (flatbed and film); drawing tablets, which work with a stylus-type pen instead of a mouse; digital cameras (often used to help create photo-realistic textures for 3-D objects); and motion-capture equipment.

Animator

This category includes 3-D modelers and 3-D artists. Modelers sculpt anything and everything that will appear in the game with regard to people, buildings, creatures, and other objects. They typically start with a concept sketch (think of it as a rough draft of the piece of art) and then build a 3-D wireframe model of the particular object. Then a texture is applied to the model. If the object is not going to be animated, the modeler's job typically ends there. If the object is going to be animated, however, it goes to the 3-D animator.

Animation can be a challenging job indeed. Not only do mechanical objects need to move realistically, but so, too, do the figures and creatures that walk, run, jump, fly, fight, and so on. This is where the job can be especially challenging. First, the animator creates an armature—the skeletal structure that defines how a 3-D model should be animated. This includes how the joints should move and how they are related hierarchically. For example, in order for a character to turn and look at something, the position of the head is dependent on the position of the neck, which is dependent on the position of the torso. And there are other details to that must be included: If the character is wearing a scarf, for example, it must blow back convincingly in the wind as he or she runs.

Two-dimensional artists, on the other hand, create textures, backgrounds, nonplaying characters, level storyboards, and other art and animations in support of the (usual) 3-D game. This person often works closely with 3-D animators to ensure that all the aesthetic components of the game come together as needed. Three-dimensional animators and modelers can make anywhere from $40,000 to $75,000; 2-D artists typically make $25,000 to $40,000 a year.

Art Director

The art director is responsible for establishing and ensuring the overall look and feel of the game, which can include determining which technology will serve a game best (2-D or 3-D) and understanding and anticipating any ramifications this decision will have. For example, the producer may want to create the game using 3-D technology, but the art director understands that based on the game's concept and design, it is cheaper and just as effective to create the game in 2-D; 3-D would be overkill. The art director will also create conceptual drawings to establish the game's basic direction and vision, assist in the recruiting and hiring of artists (including external vendors), and ensure that all artists understand the technological limitations of the software they use, among other things. Salaries range from $75,000 to $100,000, depending on experience.

Art Technician

This person is responsible for taking the thousands and thousands of graphics files created in the course of animating a game and processing them into an appropriate format so that they can be incorporated into the game. But this does not mean that any old art file will be included. The art technician helps ensure that the art looks the best it possibly can by cropping, formatting, and resizing it, as well as manipulating color to ensure the highest-possible color depth that the technology can support.

Junior Artist

Typically an entry-level position, this person works under the direction of the lead artist and supports the other members of the art team as needed while building his or her skill set and gaining valuable experience. Responsibilities can range from large to small, depending on the junior artist's skills, the size of the team, and where he or she is needed during the course of a project.

Lead Artist

The lead artist works closely with the art director, acting as his or her right-hand man. As the associate producer is to the producer, so, too, is the lead artist to the art director. This person often handles tasks such as modeling, texturing, and lighting. The lead artist is supremely comfortable with all aspect of art creation—both traditional and software—and is proficient in a wide variety of areas. This frees up the art director so that he or she can focus on driving the aesthetic direction of the game and see that it stays on track.

Audio

So while you can probably have a video game without any sound, it is just not as much fun to play. Sound and music has an important role in video games. Just as the art in a video game has an effect on how the game is received and perceived, so, too, does the music create a certain feel for a game. In fact, the MTV Video Game Awards includes a category for Best Video Game Soundtrack (surely the Academy Awards will soon follow suit!). Sound can also be a detriment to a game. As the authors of *Game Plan* state, "With the global nature of many video games, the quality of the voice acting across multiple languages can influence the success of many games. It is not uncommon to see an otherwise great game get slammed for having such a dismal voice-over that it actually ruins the gaming experience."

The successful member of the sound team has an ear for sound— yes, that sounds obvious, but think about it: Various sounds must be mixed together so that they sound exactly like the final result. The sound of a bullet hitting someone sounds different from a sword thrust, which sounds different from a fist. The successful sound engineer knows how to create these and many other sounds, and coordinate them with what is appearing on the screen.

Composer

The composer is responsible for overseeing and creating any original music employed in the game. This person has a strong background in actually playing at least one instrument, but is also well versed in the equipment and software used to digitally create music. Since much music is created using a synthesizer, people who are proficient playing and composing music on the piano may have an advantage in this profession. Successful game composers, as the authors of *Game Plan* point out, "have the ability to operate in a fluid work environment and create compositions that can work in real-time, dynamic game environments."

Sound Designer

This person is responsible for overseeing and designing the audio aspects of the game. (The creation of original music, however, is typically handled by the composer.) As with the art director and the lead designer, part of the sound designer's job is ensuring that the vision and concept of the video game is adhered to as it relates to sound. For example, in a game like *Shivers*, part of what made the game so exciting was the ambient background sounds and spot-on sound effects. The successful sound designer knows how to create sounds that, when combined with the art, add up to a truly compelling game.

Sound Effects Designer

Similar to an art technician, this person is charged with creating and processing the thousands and thousands of sound files used in the game (and make no mistake—there are a ton of them!). This position is more specialized than the sound designer—the sound effects designer is not really a lead position the way the sound designer is. Rather, the sound effects designer is responsible for—you guessed it—sound effects and only sound effects. However, at some companies, this person also directs and assists with voice-over recordings and Foley artists. In addition, the sound effects designer may work with the asset manger to catalog and track all versions of sound effects as they move through the game creation process.

Nontechnical Jobs

So not everyone at a video game developer or publisher is actually involved in the process of making a game, yet these nontechnical positions are still vital to the company's (and the game's) success. There are people who know how to make games that blow the doors off the competition, and there are people who know how to run a business like a well-oiled machine. Granted, it helps to have at least an appreciation (if not a passion) for games if you are going to work at a gaming company in any capacity. Furthermore, starting in a nontechnical position may be the "in" you need to work your way up the ladder.

Business/Legal Affairs

This department deals with contracts, licenses, and other legal matters. Often composed of lawyers, this team may also include people with experience in product or company acquisitions. A typical game requires contracts relating to all sorts of things—permissions, non-disclosure agreements, recording contracts, contracts with vendors and distributors—and the business/legal affairs department makes sure that all the t's are crossed and all the i's are dotted.

Chief Executive Officer (CEO)

This is the person responsible for the overall health of the company and—whether for good or ill—is often associated with the image of the company. Some CEOs are very hands-on, preferring to know what is going on with all areas of the company. Others are more hands-off, preferring to let the people they hired carry out the jobs they are supposed to do. And while the CEO may not have any direct experience with video games, or even care about them all that much, as the authors of *Game Plan* point out, he or she is at least smart enough to hire people who are extremely passionate and knowledgeable about video games.

Chief Financial Officer (CFO)

If you are going to develop or publish video games, you are going to need money—a lot of money. For starters, there are the people you need to hire—talented people who know what their skills are worth. Then there is the cutting-edge software and hardware you need so that the art, programming, and design departments can create cutting-edge games. Marketing and licenses cost money, too. Throw in the general overhead of running a business—rent, utilities, office supplies, and so on—and it is no surprise that it takes an enormous amount of capital to fund a video game company and keep it viable. The person that task falls to is the CFO. This person typically has a background in accounting, and has a proven track record with other companies. However, given the nature of video games, this person also is not afraid to take a calculated risk in order to see potentially monumental games.

Chief Technology Officer (CTO)

This position is similar in duties and scope to a CEO, but with a focus on leveraging monetary, intellectual, or political capital into technology to further a company's objectives or goals. This person often oversees technical staff and is tasked with deciding which platforms a game will support, what technology trends will affect the company—both now and in the future—and deciding whether to create proprietary software, like a game engine, or licensing one from a vendor. In many cases, this person has a programming background, and may have even risen through the ranks to attain this lofty position.

Customer Support

Games need players, and sometimes those players need help. That is where customer support staff step in. Smaller or start-up game companies may have their own customer support department, but as a company grows, this department is typically outsourced to an outside company. This department is actually linked to testing and quality assurance. A game that is well designed, free of bugs, and solidly put together will naturally have fewer issues and require less support than a game that was created with less attention to detail. Jim Tso, producer for LucasArts, believes that "starting out in customer support is a great way to develop problem-solving and communication skills necessary to become a producer. Since you are in direct contact with customers, these types of jobs also provide valuable insight into how customers play games and the common types of problems they run into."

Head of Studios

Larry Goldberg, head of studios at Activision Studios, describes his job as follows: "The head of studios decides which developers work on what games and, along with the president and head of publishing, decides on what games the company will make. He or she is responsible for the slate of games and making sure that the games are on time, on budget, and of high quality." Also known as vice president of production or vice president of development, this is a demanding job, since this person must oversee all issues relating to making and selling a game—all issues. The head of studios manages large groups of people, is responsible for tracking the huge budgets supporting the video game, and monitors a dizzying array of schedules.

Information Systems

People in this field operate, test, manage, and support the computer systems and networks that keep the video game company running. The information systems director is the person in charge of planning for and supervising all information systems departments in an organization. This includes developing IT-related budgets, expansion plans, strategic plans, and more. They often work with managers in other departments to set organization-wide standards with regard to equipment, training, and other practices, as well as to devise ways of using computer technology to provide better service and better meet the company's goals.

Marketing

Just as with any field, people who choose to focus on marketing become a knowledgeable expert in a given domain—in this case, video games (they may very well be avid gamers). Marketing specialists study this industry, identifying possible new markets; creating brochures and other display material; performing demonstrations at trade shows and conferences; and using surveys, focus groups, and other forms of feedback to determine if customers' needs are being met and how a game can be improved. People generally enter this field as an assistant, become a specialist or focus on research, then become an assistant marketing manager or product manager, before becoming the manager of a marketing department.

Quality Assurance

A quality assurance (QA) specialist is responsible for testing and evaluating the games to make sure they work correctly and meet the required specifications. They support programmers, who are focused more on the inner workings of a game and who do not always anticipate ways in which users will actually use a program. In a sense, programmers are depending on QA specialists to find the bugs they—and the testers—missed. These people may also suggest ways a particular game can be improved. QA specialists often start at a trainee level and then become a specialist. The more experienced specialists are promoted to a senior-level position. This person could be someone who has crossed over from a technical support or help-desk job.

Sales

Without the sales department, it is possible that the cutting-edge game that everyone has worked so hard to create will just sit in a

warehouse, gathering dust. People who work in sales have relationships with distributors and retailers, and they work these relationships hard, fighting for shelf space in retail stores. Games must sell
in huge quantities and they must do so fast, and it is the job of the
sales department to see that this happens.

Chapter 4

Tips for Success

You have your foot in the door in the video game industry, but how do you keep your career on track? How is this track even determined? What are the best ways to advance in this career? What are the quickest ways to undermine it?

Throughout this book, interview candidates have offered valuable advice in this regard. This chapter will address these questions in more detail, with specific tips and techniques, including what qualities set candidates apart, and more. Tips for success relating to specific positions are included, but they can be applied to similar occupations. Tips for an occupation that is not specifically mentioned here can be extrapolated by looking at a related position. For example, someone who works as a programmer may find the tips given for a designer or tester to be equally valuable.

In addition, people often do not stay in the position or group that they begin their career in. As with most fields these days, changing jobs is often an important way of furthering one's career. This makes sense when you consider the importance of staying abreast of the technology, anticipating changes and trends in the video game industry where possible, and moving to take advantage of them. The same experience, credentials, and traits that will help you advance your career by getting a job at a different company also are likely to help you get promoted within a company.

Establishing a Professional Reputation

Regardless of how casual your work environment is or how small the company may be, there is no excuse for not acting professionally. If you do not take your career seriously, no one else will. There are things that can firmly establish you as a professional, and there are things that can quickly ruin your reputation.

From a technology standpoint, you can establish yourself as a professional by staying up-to-date on what is happening in the industry. Stay abreast of technological innovations and progress, as well as the processes and tools available. Use the simplest solution possible to meet a project's requirements.

From a computing standpoint, it is important to recognize your limits. One of the easiest ways to ruin your reputation is to get in over your head on something and destroy a customer's computing environment. Computer management tools exist that could allow a person to do this without even realizing it.

Another of the quickest ways you can ruin your professional reputation is by using negative comments. Avoid words like *don't, won't,* and *can't*. For example, rather than saying "I don't work well with negative people," say, "I find working with negative people an enjoyable challenge, although it can be tough and I would like to avoid it if possible." The first statement implies that you are not adaptable and are unable to work with a variety of people. The latter statement shows that you are flexible and willing to tackle difficult situations.

Another reputation-killer is to have people think you are unreliable or picky about the type of work you are willing to do. Again, this goes back to *don't* versus *didn't*. For example, rather than saying that you "don't" do project management, say you "didn't" do project management in your last job but would be willing to try it with guidance where needed.

Be a person who does things and gets things done. Be proactive—look for what needs to be done and be prepared to do whatever it takes to help. Work that you are responsible for should be the highest quality and should be completed on time.

Honesty and accountability also go a long way in establishing a professional reputation. If you did not do a good job on something, be honest about it. Trying to blame someone else for problems you encountered or as an excuse for the state of your work, or just producing work of low quality when you (and perhaps your boss) knows you are capable of more, will be noticed and remembered. Just as attention to detail is a key skill for many positions in the computing industry, so is it a factor when it comes to one's professional reputation.

The Value of Networking

There is truth in the old adage, "It is not what you know, it is *who* you know," although it does not necessarily mean what you might think at first when applied to the video game industry. This is a young, ambitious field, not an old, established one, and results are still the most important thing. People who can do the work and do it darn well are going to win out over those who "happen to know someone in the field" most of the time. The video game field is too competitive for slackers to survive long—provided they even manage to get a job on connections alone in the first place. However, connections are still important. As mentioned, jobs in this field are highly sought after, and those who have successful careers in the video game industry do so partly because they know where the jobs are and where to meet the people who can help them land those jobs.

This is where networking comes in. According to author Ernest Adams, professional contacts are one of the most important business resources for people in this field. He states, "This is one of the reasons that professional conferences and trade shows have so many parties ...The companies throwing these parties ...are doing it to get their employees together with new people: to renew old relationships and make new ones." Lee Rossini, director of marketing for Sierra Entertainment, echoes this sentiment: "Make a friend in the industry," he says, "It is just too tough to get in without one ...Get in any way you can, prove yourself, and start going after the job you really want once you are on board."

So where does one find these friends and connections? Chapter 6 has a list of several trade groups and associations for various areas of the video game industry. Other tips include:

➡ Read magazines and Web sites that pertain to your area of interest, and participate in online forums and chat groups. People in the game industry like to share their knowledge. Use your real name when participating in discussions, and be professional. If you are new to the field, do not be afraid to admit it. Avoid flame wars—they serve absolutely no purpose. Be open-minded to any ideas someone may have, and share your own insights and information when possible.

➡ Join a local chapter for the organization or association in your area, if possible. If there is no local chapter in your area, consider starting one. The International Game Developers Association (IGDA), for example, has chapters throughout the world, and they often have meetings once a month or so.

➡ Go to conferences and trade shows. While this piece of networking advice is also the most costly one, if you have the money, it is money well spent. It gives you the most exposure to the most people all at once. Chapter 2 provides overviews of several notable conferences and trade shows for people in the video game field.

Problem
Solving

A common problem players of RPGs and MMOGs experience is the player who goes around making life miserable for everyone else just trying to complete a quest. Recall the *South Park* episode "Make Love, Not Warcraft" where a rogue player wandered throughout the game, killing everyone he came across, and you will understand how frustrating this problem can be. These players take great delight in tormenting players to the point where they give up the game in frustration.

So what is a developer to do? Clearly, the problem must be anticipated and addressed. These players, known as griefers or PKers (player killers) cannot be ignored in the hope they will get bored and go away. Instead, your regular subscribers will leave. Nor is it effective in terms of time and cost to try and ban these players—they can just create new characters under new account names and continue to wreak havoc. Some developers believe that griefers actually enhance game play by providing additional, unexpected challenges and use these players to their advantage, creating a game system that allows griefers to do their thing in some areas but not in others. *World of Warcraft*, for example, has a system whereby players can flag themselves as being open to both attack and to be attacked by other players.

When Considering a Move

The video game industry can be looked at as having three different career ladders: development, production, and game design. This is not the same as an organizational chart. Rather, it is a path that shows the typical path to advancement a person in a given ladder takes as skills and experience are acquired. The development ladder comprises programming, art, and sound. People typically start at a junior or associate level and work their way up. The work often does not change as a person moves up the development ladder, but there are more responsibilities and more important tasks.

With the production ladder, on the other hand, advancement is not based on technical or creative prowess—rather, it is based on qualities like leadership, organization, management, product sense, and so on. This ladder typically starts with testing, then moves to quality assurance, then assistant producer and up the rungs to the CEO. If you have a passion for the gaming industry but do not consider yourself to be a particularly creative person, this may be the ladder for you.

The design ladder starts with a level designer or world builder position and moves up to game designer, creative director, and ultimately chief creative officer. The duties and responsibilities can change as a person moves up the ladder. Design is not always a third career ladder unto itself. Sometimes it is part of production, and sometimes it is part of development, depending on the particular company. Therefore, it is often easier to make the switch from design to one of the other two ladders.

People who see success in this field can learn and work with little supervision, possess good communication skills (both in speaking and writing), are analytical yet creative thinkers, and can adapt to the ever-changing trends in this industry. People move up in this industry based largely on their performance and proficiency—as a person's skill level improves, so, too, does their position in most cases. Time and experience often equal better job opportunities. Moving from one particular aspect of the video game industry, however, to another—for example, from animation to music—can be harder to pull off, but it can be done. It may mean that you have to learn new skills, and it may mean that you have to take a step down the career ladder in relation to where you are now, but if the opportunity presents itself and it is something you really want, then make the switch. It is not likely that the position a person starts out with in this field is the one he or she remains in throughout their career. Interests change, career paths open up, or the entry-level job is merely a stepping stone to a larger career goal. When looking to make a career move—whether vertically or laterally—consider the following.

Identify Your Key Skills

Your "key skills" include the ones that are related to the job you are seeking. For example, knowledge of certain programming languages, experience with design programs, or a stint as a beta tester are all practical skills relevant to a career in the video game industry. Job-related skills such as these are often (but not always) in line with the path on which you plan to take your career.

Then there are the skills that make you a good worker. Regardless of the field, there are certain skills that most employers look for in an applicant, such as promptness, reliability, diligence, and work ethic. These are the skills that do not have anything to do with the specific job—or with any job, for that matter—but make a person well suited for a particular career. For example, many jobs in the video game field are ideal for people who are detail-oriented, creative, and—of course—who enjoy playing games.

Finally, there are transferrable skills—these skills may not have anything to do with video games, per se, but they can certainly help you in that line of work. For example, a person who has experience in the fine arts might do well as an animator. A person who has experience in retail sales might find those skills transfer well to a support position. A person with a pitch-perfect ear may find creating music soundtracks for games enables him or her to utilize those skills on another level.

Define Your Ideal Job

Your ideal job is more than just a title. When clarifying this in your mind, consider things like the skills you feel you are strongest in and that you want to utilize (or perhaps skills you do not yet possess but want to become proficient in—by developing those skills you can further advance your career!). Consider the work environment you would find ideal: working at home, working for a small company, working for a large company, working a traditional 40-hour-a-week job, working whatever hours a job requires, or perhaps being on call. The environment also extends to the people. Those who want to be surrounded by people who are more creative might be better suited working for in gaming. Those who are passionate about giving back to the community may find themselves drawn to a nonprofit that specializes in creating educational games for use in schools. Location is another factor to consider. Do you want to work in a particular city, such as Seattle, San Diego, or Singapore? Have you had enough of winters in Minnesota and decided that life in Florida is better suited for you? And then there's income. Some people want to make $100,000 a year; for others, $40,000 is sufficient. Keep in mind that you may have to start with the $40,000 salary to get to the $100,000 one.

Be proactive when it comes to your career. Do not just wing it and hope for the best. If you want to succeed, you must have a plan. If you do not have one, find a mentor—whether a manager, another co-worker, or a supervisor—and ask them for advice. However, before latching onto one, you need to think about this person's skills and way of working, and be sure that you do indeed desire to be more like him or her. Keep in mind that if you work with a mentor, others will associate you with this person. That can be a great thing, but it can backfire on you, too. For example, if the person you are considering as a mentor is considered brilliant, but difficult to work with, you may acquire the same reputation.

Things That Can Make or Break Your Interview

Books and Web sites abound with information on the do's and don'ts of interviewing, and while most of that information will not be repeated here, a few points do bear repeating, with an emphasis on how they can help advance a career in video games. What you wear really does matter. Even if the corporate culture at the company is casual and laid back with regard to work attire, that does not mean you should dress that way for your interview. You do not necessarily need to wear a business suit, but your clothes should be clean and wrinkle-free, with no rips or tears. Wear slacks rather than jeans.

Make eye contact when you first meet the person who greets you for your interview, once or twice again while walking to the interview location, and again when you first sit down to do the interview. Shake the person's hand firmly. Act professional and confident. Before the interview, read up on the company, the business, and the business group. Investigate the company and the position as thoroughly as you can. Write down at least five questions that you can ask in the interview. If you really want to land a job, be as prepared for the interview as you can. The fact that you have questions may be what sets you apart. In addition, along with thoroughly understanding everything you can about the position you are applying for, know how to position your current skills against the job you are after. If you are an artist or composer, bring a portfolio of your best work and ask ahead of time which format the interviewer would prefer (CD, DVD, or traditional format). If you are a developer or tester, be prepared to discuss code questions (and to provide answers!); also be prepared to discuss your contribution to recent projects.

Author Ernest Adams emphasizes that the game industry is heavily driven by environment, so it is important to get a feel for the people, the company's culture, and the corporate structure. Thus, he recommends asking the following questions during an interview:

➡ Is there anything you wish you had known before you came to work here?

➡ Describe the corporate culture to me.

➡ Tell me about a recent internal event that made an impact on the company.

➡ Describe some of your star performers to me.

➡ When top performers leave, why do they leave and where do they go?

➡ What are the biggest problems facing this department over the next two years?

➡ What does the company plan to do over the next year to make things better?

➡ If you were my best friend, what you would tell me about this job that you have not already said?

Résumés and Cover Letters

As with interviewing, many, many books, articles, and Web sites abound with information on how to craft a cover letter and résumé that gets results. This book will not repeat those here. It will, however, offer a reminder of tips that apply to the video game industry. They come from Mary Margaret Walker, owner of a recruitment and business services firm (http://www.mary-margaret.com) that works with a wide range of clients in the game, mobile, web, multimedia, IT, TV, and film industries. She offers the following résumé tips:

➡ In the experience section, list your previous employers, your job title with those employers, and your dates of employment, with your most recent experience first.

➡ Rather than using paragraphs, create bullet lists of your tasks and accomplishments. Include the titles of games you have worked on and your role in those games.

➡ In the education section, note the school and degree awarded.

➡ Present your qualifications in a powerful, enticing, easy-to-read manner.

➡ Do not list your age or date of birth on a résumé meant for U.S. employers.

➡ If you are female and concerned about possible gender discrimination, you could use your initials rather than your first name (E.M. Charles, for example, rather than Elizabeth Charles).

➡ Do not list your salary history on your résumé. You can provide this information later, if asked for it.

➡ You do not need to state that references are available upon request. Either go ahead and include a list of references or wait to be asked for them.

➡ It is not necessary to list jobs that are older than 10 or 15 years, especially if they are not relevant to the video game field.

Tips that Mary Margaret Walker offers with respect to cover letters include:

➡ Politely introduce yourself and present your résumé. Explain how you heard about the job, why you believe you are a good fit for it, and end with a request for an interview or further communication.

➡ Rewrite the cover letter for each company you send it to. Include content that shows you know something about the company.

➡ Be confident, but not arrogant. The objective is to land an interview and make the person reading your cover letter want to meet you in person.

➡️ Formal politeness is necessary. If, for example, the name of the contact person for the job is Sarah Brown, address the letter to "Dear Ms. Brown," not "Dear Sarah." It is best to address the letter to a specific person; if that is not possible, you can use "Dear Sir or Madam."

➡️ Use proper English and avoid slang, text-messaging short-cuts, and online speak. Standard game industry acronyms can be used, such as RPG and MMOG.

➡️ Keep the letter to one-half to three-quarters of a page in length,

➡️ Double-check your spelling and grammar, and then check it again. One handy trick: Read your letter (and résumé, for that matter) backwards. Your eye is more likely to catch things you are not expecting to see.

The Portfolio

Those who are new to the game industry—even those who are still relatively new to it—will quickly realize that the only way you are going to land any kind of a skill-based job is to have a portfolio. Also called a demo or a reel, this is a sampling of the best work you have done. Professional artists and animators have them, for sure, but so, too, at times, do composers and programmers. You cannot expect to break into this field without one. Tips that Mary Margaret Walker offers with regard to portfolios include:

➡️ Have your portfolio in as many different formats as possible. Some employers want these in CD or DVD format—some even still want them in VHS. The particularly savvy job candidate will even have the portfolio available on a Web site.

➡️ Deliver your portfolio exactly how the interviewer requests it. Fail to follow this step, and your application could get rejected outright, no matter how great the content it contains.

➡️ If your portfolio is on a CD, test it on different computers and operating systems to make sure that it will work.

➡️ Always include a credits list and a shot list. A credits list is a list of the people (even if that is just you) who contributed to a particular project. A shot list is the list of scenes in a demo, in sequence, including camera angles. It is like a storyboard without the pictures.

➡ Make sure your portfolio shows a wide range of your talents and skills rather than focusing on one specific area.

➡ Display as many different genres and art styles in your portfolio as possible. If you have only worked on one kind of game, seek out the necessary experience to expand your portfolio (you will expand your skill set at the same time).

➡ A portfolio that plays automatically, like on a Web site, should not run more than three or four minutes and should feature your best work first; a portfolio that you present in person should not be longer than 10 minutes.

➡ Think of your portfolio as an extension of your résumé. That means tweaking it for the specific company for whom you are interviewing and make sure it highlights your best, most salient work for the position at hand.

Defining a Career Path

Sometimes, a person enters this field with a specific career path in mind; for others, the path evolves as the career evolves. Both approaches are fine—the key is to be flexible but deliberate. In general, the basic career path that people in this field follow is to start with a degree from a technical college or a bachelor's degree in computer science or fine arts and then to follow that with industry certification (if necessary and relevant), depending on your area of specific interest. Chapter 3 provides an in-depth look at how certain positions are related and common ways to move up and among these jobs.

Design is often considered the "sexiest" job in the video game industry, but not everyone is able to jump right into that career path (indeed, some have no interest in that area at all). One of the most common paths is to start in quality assurance. Chapter 3 explained this position in more detail; it essentially involves making sure that a game works as a piece of software—it does what it is supposed to. Other paths include assistant designer and associate producer (again, see chapter 3 for more information). According to Matt Harding, lead designer at Pandemic Studios, all good designers possess four key qualities: (1) They are prolific, in that they can turn a product out and move on to the next one (which is harder than you might think!); (2) they are structured, in that they make a set of rules for their games and stick with them; (3) they are articulate, in that they can communicate clearly and listen to others' criticism, processing it objectively and responding; and (4) most importantly, they are fun, in that they know that putting a tree, for example, in one place is better than putting it in another place. They may not be able to articulate why this is so, but they just know that it is. And they are right!

The most successful writers in the gaming industry, as mentioned in chapter 3, are often freelance writers rather than full-time employees, especially when licensed franchise titles are involved, such as *Star Wars* or *Spider-Man*. Ray DeLaurentis, writer for Jim Henson Productions and Disney Interactive has the following advice for those who wish to write for video games: "First master your craft as a conventional writer. You cannot break the rules before you learn them. And if conventional writing is like giving people a guided tour of your home, writing for games is like handing over your keys and letting them rummage through your house without you—a much scarier and more thrilling proposition."

A beta tester is someone who helps video game publishers identify weak points in their products, which could cause frustration for players. This person also identifies specific issues that need to be corrected before a product can be released. Typically, beta testers test several incarnations of a product, until it is deemed ready for release. Beta testing is a great way to get your foot in the door with a video game company. Publishers of video games often advertise on their sites that they are looking for outside beta testers. There are two types of beta tests: open, in which anyone is allowed to download and play a particular game, and closed, in which the

Fast Facts

What is in a name? The term Pac-Man comes from the Japanese word *paku paku*, which is Japanese onomatopoeia for noisy eating (similar to *chomp chomp*). The game was released in Japan with the name *Puck-Man*, but released in the United States with the name *Pac-Man*, fearing kids might deface a Puck-Man cabinet by changing the P to an F.

publisher selects a group of testers from among a group of applicants. It is better to get in on a closed beta test instead of an open one. The quality bar is higher in a closed test. As Ernest Adams points out in his book *Breaking into the Game Industry*, "with closed beta testing, the company hopes to find people who are serious and dedicated to helping them make a better game." If you are one of these people and you hit it off with the testing manager, you may find yourself getting called back for other beta tests, which could be the first step in your career in the video game industry.

As far as production goes, the most successful producers are multitasking gurus—able to juggle dozens of complex tasks without missing a thing, while staying on top of budgetary constraints and schedule deadlines. Often, one of the surest ways to advance in this path is through networking. Producers, whether at the assistant or lead level, often work with team members in different departments. Those connections may come in handy when looking to move from production to design, for example.

Programmers, as has been made clear by now, are the people behind the scenes, as it were. They take the ideas from the designer and bring them to life. According to Dr. Ian Lane Davis, CEO of Mad Doc Software, "A lead programmer needs to be able to architect a good engine, manage programmers, and communicate with the other team members. You can find a person with one of these qualities, but it is extremely rare to find a person with all three." Thus, anyone looking to move up the programming ladder would be advised to hone all three of those qualities.

But What About the Long Hours?

You've heard the rumors: teams pull all-nighters to ensure that a crucial deadline is met so that a game can release on time. Members stay in the office for days on end, only coming home to maybe shower and grab a couple of hours sleep. They live on a diet of takeout and Mountain Dew. Well, the rumors are true—and they may even be worse than you think. Creating fun is hard work. However, the good news is that the insane hours are not constant. The video game industry is a cyclical one, and projects are often coordinated so that they release in time for summer and Christmas. For the most part, work hours are regular—around 50 or so hours a week, five or six days a week. But then, invariably, things happen during a project's development—maybe a certain piece of technology is not

Keeping
in Touch

Sort of like a Facebook for the business world, LinkedIn (http://www.linkedin.com) "is an interconnected network of experienced professionals from around the world, representing 170 industries and 200 countries. You can find, be introduced to, and collaborate with qualified professionals that you need to work with to accomplish your goals." According to their site, LinkedIn has over 35 million members in over 200 countries and territories around the world; a new member joins LinkedIn approximately every second, and about half of the members are outside the United States; and executives from all Fortune 500 companies are LinkedIn members. Overall, the site has immense value as a networking tool. One member notes, "You have to spend some time and effort to build your network and search to find the right people. But the great thing is that those efforts are multiplied over and over by the slick LinkedIn system."

working as expected, or there is a flaw in the game's design, or maybe there was a management issue higher up and that has trickled down to affect the project. Whatever the cause, the problem is now yours (and likely your whole team's, of course). It is time to go to bat.

These periods—although brief—can be brutal and often occur right before a critical milestone in the project or before the final code release. Forget about weekends, vacations, and anything approaching a decent night's sleep. While these occasions are practically inevitable (and, as mentioned, in most companies, this is not the norm), there are things you can do to help make life more bearable during such times. Authors Alan Gershenfeld, Mark Loparco, and Cecilia Barajas recommend the following in their book, *Game Plan*.

Avoid "Death March" Cultures

Believe it or not, some companies actually brag about the insane hours their teams are expected to keep. Yes, long hours are standard in this industry, but insane, outrageous ones typically are not. Unfortunately, if this is not something you investigated before taking a job at a company, you may be stuck—that is, until you can find

INTERVIEW

How Professionalism Can Advance Your Career

Todd MacIntyre
Senior Producer, Big Blue Bubble

What is the best way to quickly establish a professional reputation? What is the easiest way to trash this reputation?
The quickest way to establish a reputation within a company is to be a team player. Tasks within game development rely so much on other people that you need to make sure you are keeping the rest of team in mind when doing your work. You do not have the freedom to just get things done when you feel like doing them. [Considering] the rest of your team will show everyone you are a professional. Also, keeping open-minded about how they run things around the office will show a big sense of professionalism. [Other groups'] processes might not be the best way to do things, but the company has been doing it that way for a reason, and to go into a company and immediately tell them they are doing things "wrong" and trying to restructure it is a way to get on the wrong side of things. [However,] suggesting ways (without being confrontational) that things can be improved is something every company wants to do ...and suggesting improvements and alternate ways of doing things shows initiative and interest in the company, and is a way to establish a professional reputation without coming in and shaking things up.

The quickest way to ruin a reputation is to not take your work seriously. Yes, the game industry is one that is more relaxed than most out there and is renowned for not following the typical working environment formula, but people still need to remember that even though a studio may feel like you are in a university dorm, it is also a serious industry and deadlines are tight and a lot of money is involved. Employees need to be able to work in a fun environment while also being serious about the work they are doing. You cannot afford the time to casually fix a few bugs when you are approaching an alpha or beta deadline, and sometimes you have to say no to that "after-work session of *Halo*" so you can get your work done because the programmer you are working with cannot proceed unless he or she has your art, or the designer cannot get that setup finalized until some code has been done. Everyone's work is intertwined with each other's, so you need to be able to work as a fellow teammate and not have the idea that you work in a bubble.

What do you consider the biggest myth about the video game industry, if any?

The biggest myth about the video game industry is that we play games all day. This is a fun job; however, it is nonetheless still "a job." Game development has its relaxed atmosphere (which varies from place to place), but this is not a position where you leisurely just sit and play games all day. This is a serious business with lots of competition and secrecy around it, and many people just getting into the industry are shell-shocked about the fact that they are not just sitting down and playing a fun round of a game every day. There is a lot of serious work involved and high-pressure moments to meet deadlines, fix elusive bugs, optimize assets so the engine runs at the right frame rate, etc.

What are some common problems in this industry and how do you think they could be improved?

1. This is a very competitive industry, and developers keep their ideas and technology secretive so they can keep the upper hand on competitive products. This is understandable, but at the same time, in order for the industry to grow, mature, and improve, there has to be some sharing of ideas so we can all work together to improve the industry. It is a slippery slope, but it is starting to make ground at events like GDC (Game Developers Conference) where they have round table discussions on various industry topics.

2. There is always the desire to elicit excitement in consumers and the media in order to generate sales and notoriety in a product. But many developers/publishers have a tendency to do this too early and the hype machine gets rolling, only to be disappointed [whether] by promises that were not kept (because of technical issues), expectations were not met, or the project never surfaced. We need to learn to hold our cards close to our chest for a little bit and not jump the gun to make announcements about projects that are barely started, and the media needs to learn that they will get better previews and content if they just remain patient and wait for the projects to be more complete before demanding exclusives.

3. Training needs to be drastically improved. There are more and more institutions that are opening training geared towards game development, but many of them seem to be last-minute thoughts and are not integrated enough to teach students what they need to know. We need professionals who are willing to

(continues on next page)

INTERVIEW

How Professionalism Can Advance Your Career
(continued)

devote their time to teaching these skills instead of just being a full-time developer and part-time teacher, and we need the institutions to take the industry serious enough to make a solid and reliable curriculum that is devoted to giving students the knowledge they need. This is getting better, but it still has a ways to go.

4. The games industry needs a higher female presence. There are many game players out there who are female, but the majority still need to understand that they can contribute just as much to game design (and in many cases more) than the male population. The art area of games is quite well represented, and the programming section has seen some big increases in female coders, but the game design sector still needs much more female representation in order to get a different perspective on how

a new job. When researching companies, talk to people about typical work schedules. Ask about the working environment. After all, you are going to be spending a good chunk of your days here, so you ought to know what you signed up for. On the other hand, if you are kind of person who thrives on such a crazy work schedule and never wanted a life in the first place, well then, work on! Just be prepared for the consequences.

Look for Teams with Experience

In general, it is the team with experience who suffers the least when a project slips. These are the veterans who know that things can (and often do) go wrong, and they build time into their project schedules to account for such contingencies. They have been around the block a few times and worked on their share of games. These valuable team members know what problems to anticipate, how to avoid them, and what to do if such problems occur. However, there is that saying about best laid plans. Sometimes things happen that players can play a game. This is the one area that would benefit the most (more than art and code) to have a female perspective on how a game is structured.

Is there anything else a person new to this industry should know?

Anyone who wants to be in game development needs to make sure they are educated on all the games that are on the market. You need to be familiar with everything that your customer has available to them. Even though you love to play games and make them, you need to strike a good balance between making a game that you like and that you are happy with and making sure you are creating something that is appealing to your target demographic. Putting in blood effects because you think they are cool is not going to appeal to a young player target demographic if that is who your objective is.

Make sure you take pride in the projects you work on, regardless if it is something you would normally play or not. It will make the whole process more enjoyable, and you will learn more if you are invested in the project. You will be surprised what you can learn making or playing games that are not something you would normally play.

are beyond anyone's control and no one anticipated them, or maybe you are not fortunate enough to work on such an experienced team. Consider this project a learning experience. As the authors of *Game Plan* state, "Often you can learn more from a poorly run project than a smooth project—just do not make the same mistake twice."

Look for Strong, Qualified Leaders

This tip goes hand in hand with finding a team with experience. Such leadership may be what makes or breaks a game. The team lead is the person who does just that. He or she is responsible for keeping the game on track, both creatively and logistically. Because many games today are large, complex ventures, typically, there is a team lead for each division: a team lead for the software programming, a team lead for animation, a team lead for design, one for music, and so on. Strong qualified leaders know the importance of communicating with all members of the team, and often. They understand not only their role but the roles of everyone else. For example, the artist understands the technical needs of the programmers and prepares the art accordingly. The sound designer understands the memory limitations allotted for sound and creates sound files to fit within those needs. Strong leaders understand that everyone's job is important and that no single aspect of the game is more important than another—all are necessary to achieve a best-selling game.

Avoid Projects with Unrealistic Scopes

Project scope refers to the size and complexity of a project. As the authors of *Game Plan* state, "In the quest to create the best game ever, there is a tendency to toss in more elements ...what is often overlooked in expanding the project is that every additional element has a rippling effect on every other aspect." Great team leaders know what is realistic for a game in terms of budgetary and time constraints. While a designer might think it would be super cool to have just one more level in the game with the most evil villain ever, the design lead knows what this really involves in terms of code, art, music, and so on, and is willing to say "no" for the greater good of the project (i.e. getting that game released to market on time!). However, as the authors of *Game Plan* point out, this is not just the responsibility of team leaders. Every single person involved in the project needs to always keep an eye towards what is realistic and feasible in terms of time and money.

Look for Good, Solid Technology

At its heart, a video game is just a piece of software. That software must be thoroughly understood—both in terms of what it can do and what it cannot do. In fact, the limitations of software may be more important than its capabilities because that is another constraint. There is no point in designing a game with features that the current software cannot support—and there is another word for people who spend time on such development without educating themselves on the software ahead of time. It is like making an offer on a house before you even know how much of a loan you are qualified for. According to the authors of *Game Plan*, "The two positions critical for avoiding technology nightmares are the lead programmer and the project manager. Ideally, the project manager should possess an understanding of the technology. A good lead programmer must not only be a good technologist [but also] a good manager."

INTERVIEW

A New Direction for the Industry?

Stan Miskiewicz
CEO, Black Point Studios

What drew you to the video games industry?
In 1992 I was living in Berlin as an editorial photographer; at that time, companies were starting to create pre-viz for reconstruction of eastern Germany, it was also the start of the Love Parade [a popular festival and parade that originated in 1989 in Berlin, Germany]. People knew me as a photographer and started to hire me as an art and creative director for both. We won some awards, and that is how I entered the industry.

What developments took you by surprise? Can you predict any new trends?
Outsourcing to Asia and India and how fast that came up was a surprise. I hope that a company like Apple would create a console and open it up like the iPhone—that would change the industry and really bring it back to its roots. China and India are not the answers. Much of the work we have done in the last years has been redoing work sent overseas. Accountants should not run the company. It is easy to see that this [current] business model of the game industry is not working—just look at the studios closing and their losses; on the other side, look at the iPhone and its success in the game field. The industry needs to open up and look to shops like ours and our intellectual property to bring back the industry. Publishers should look at putting out BBB titles. You can put out seven $8 million games instead of one money-losing AAA title. It just makes sense.

Effective Business Communication Techniques

One of the most important skills a person in this field can have is the ability to talk "gamespeak" or "techspeak" to those who might not be so knowledgeable. Learn how to explain concepts in a way that is not demeaning to the non-technical person, yet assures understanding—and do not talk down to them. Make sure the non-techies are satisfied with the explanation and all questions have been answered.

This is also important when in meetings or similar situations where, for example, a user interface designer or software developer is explaining how a game's technical requirements are greater than anticipated and require more resources sooner rather than later. Avoid slipping into overuse of jargon and acronyms. Just because you are familiar with these terms does not mean everyone else around you is. Also, this concept is important to keep in mind no matter what form your communication is in—whether face-to-face, on the phone, via e-mail or instant messaging, or a business proposal, keep your audience and their level of understanding in mind.

Managing Your Time Effectively

While sometimes a person can get in over their head because they overestimate their skills, in many cases, this occurs because of improper time management. Developing techniques and strategies that help you manage your time effectively will, in turn, reduce your stress level and increase productivity. This advice holds true for anyone, in any position, but people in the video game field— perhaps programmers and developers in particular—are especially prone to falling into this trap.

When you have projects with hard and fast deadlines, prioritize your schedule accordingly. Block out this time in your schedule if you need to, and let coworkers and others know that you need to be undisturbed for a given amount of time—even if it is just an hour. That hour of concentrated work could be worth four hours of work with interruptions. If you need to (and if this is possible, given your work environment), consider working in a separate room.

Some people are at their sharpest in the morning; others are more effective in the afternoon. Know what your "best" time of the day is and tackle your most challenging tasks then. If you still find it hard to stay on task, try to figure out where the block lies. Are you lacking information to complete the tasks? Are you lacking motivation? Are you unclear about the goals? Positively identifying some of these problem areas will often lead to solutions, which, in turn, leads to better time management.

If you find yourself chronically behind in tasks and routinely missing deadlines, for the sake of your professional reputation, consider keeping a "time diary." Just as people who are struggling with their weight or their finances keep a log for a week or a month, noting where every penny goes or what they put in their mouth, so, too, can keeping a log of where and how you are spending your time show you where simple changes can help improve efficiency. For example, a 2007 survey conducted on behalf of Fuser.com found that 87 percent of U.S. Internet users spend at least seven hours a week managing their e-mail—that is practically an entire workday!

One well-known, effective time management technique is the basic "to do" list. Every evening, before you leave work, make a list of what you need to accomplish the next day. Prioritize it in terms of urgency and importance. Aim to achieve as much as possible, but always remain flexible so that you can take on unexpected tasks if necessary.

While it is natural to want to say "yes" to everything that is asked of you, if you try to juggle too many balls in the air at once, you are bound to drop a few—and your professional reputation can suffer. If you are asked to take on a task and you know that you will not be able to meet the deadline, you must communicate that up front. Be honest—do not give a vague answer like "I'm not sure." Consider negotiating on the timing. For example, say, "I cannot do it today, but I would be happy to do it by the end of the week." If this task is one you simply cannot turn down, work with your supervisor or other colleagues, explain the situation to them, and come up with a plan so that other deadlines are not missed. Learning to say no is not easy, but you will earn more respect by understanding and respecting your own limits—and communicating them clearly and effectively—rather than saying "yes" to everything and paying the price down the road.

Chapter 5

Talk Like a Pro

Because the video game industry can be jargon-laden at times, the following in-depth glossary explains industry jargon, key terminology, phrases, concepts, and general business language that will help you hit the ground running upon launching your new career.

2-D A graphics-related term that refers to the depiction of scenery, objects, game play, etc. in two dimensions: height and width.

3-D A graphics related term that refers to the depiction of scenery, objects, game play, etc. in three dimensions: height, width, and depth. The crucial component of 3-D display—depth—is conveyed through the use of perspective and drawing techniques such as shadow or gradient. This term also applies to specialized hardware (chips and boards) designed to accelerate and enhance the display of 3-D environments by handling tasks for the CPU. This includes a processor that renders 3-D scenes and extra memory that handles fonts, textures, and more.

AAC Advanced Audio Coding. A standard compression and encoding scheme for digital audio that is designed to provide better sound quality than MP3. Gaming consoles such as the Nintendo DS and Nintendo Wii, as well as the Sony PlayStation and Sony PlayStation Portable, make use of this audio standard.

action game Any game whose challenge consists primarily of eye-hand coordination to shoot and drive accurately, time jumps and runs perfectly, and more. Not all video games are action games, contrary to popular belief.

adventure game A slower-paced game in which the player is typically in the role of a character in a world and having an adventure of some sort. As opposed to an action game, adventure games often require the player to solve puzzles using logic rather than employ motor skills. Adventure games typically have strong plotlines, well-developed worlds, and intricate scenery.

agnostic A term that refers to a software platform, application, or other device that will run on any operating system.

algorithm A procedure or formula for solving a problem. In most cases, an algorithm must end after the problem is solved.

alpha A game that is in the alpha stage of development contains all of the features necessary for play and is ready for testing. Unlike beta testing, alpha testing is done entirely internally, by the publisher, developers, and other team members.

analog As the word pertains to computing, it refers to a computer that uses continuous electrical, mechanical, or hydraulic quantities to model the problem being solved. With an analog computer, numbers are represented by directly measurable quantities, such as voltages or rotations.

application programming interface (API) A set of routines used by a program to direct the performance of procedures by an operating system. APIs can be language-dependent (utilizing the particular syntax and elements of a programming language) or language-independent (written so that they can be called from several programming languages).

armature Data that define how the skeletal structure of a 3-D model should be animated. This data includes how the joints should move and how they are related hierarchically. For example, in order for a character to turn and look at something, the position of the head is dependent on the position of the neck, which is dependent on the position of the torso.

artificial intelligence Also known simply as "AI," this field of computer science has to do with the intelligence of machines. John McCarthy, an American computer scientist, coined the term in 1956 as "the science and engineering of making intelligent machines."

assembler A device that converts assembly language code into machine code.

assembly language Low-level programming languages that used symbolic representations of numeric machine codes and other constants needed to program a particular CPU architecture—in other words, a human-readable form of a computer's internal language. Each type of processor has its own assembly language. Once the primary way in which computer games were written, assembly languages are now used mainly for optimizing speed-sensitive parts of code.

assets A collective term referring to the data files needed for a game: audio, video, animation, and more. Managing assets is an important part of any video game developer's job.

avatar A character in a game who represents and is controlled by the player. Prominent examples include characters in a first-person shooter game or the characters players can create in *Second Life*.

beta A term referring to new software or hardware that is either being updated or is ready to be released to a select group of users for testing. In beta testing, potential customer and users test the functionality of the product and report any errors found. This is typically one of the last steps in development before a product is released to market.

binary With regards to computing, this term refers to the system of representing text or program instructions through the use of a two-digit number system. Zero represents the "off" state; one represents the "on" state.

bit A piece of data represented by either a zero or a one.

box and docs A term that refers to the physical packaging, along with all the materials that go inside a game box, including game discs, documentation, game maps, and user manuals.

bug An error in computer coding or logic that causes a program to function incorrectly or to produce incorrect or unexpected results.

build The compilation of source code files into executable code. A build is not the complete game. Rather, the build is a compilation of the files needed to play the game with the features implemented to date. Builds are typically used during the testing process.

bundle To combine products for sale as one unit. For example, software programs are often bundled and offered for sale with a computer or other hardware, or several games in a series may be bundled and sold as one item. Bundling is designed to increase a product's functionality or attractiveness.

Everyone Knows

So how do publishers and distributors differ? Akin to a book publisher, a game publisher funds the development of new games and markets them to the public (who buys them from retailers). The publisher is the financial, but not necessarily the creative, center of the game industry. Publishers can develop games in-house, or they can contract out the development and have it done externally. Distributors, on the other hand, neither develop nor publish games. Rather, they act as an intermediary, selling games to retailers on behalf of publishers. Distributors are often used by smaller publishing companies, who typically do not have the financial muscle of the larger companies and cannot afford to have their own warehouse space and sales staff.

byte A byte is comprised of eight bits. These groups of 8 bits can represent up to 256 different values and can correspond to a variety of different symbols, letters or instructions.

cache A temporary storage area where frequently accessed data can be stored for rapid access. Once data is stored in the cache, it can be accessed from here rather than being retrieved or calculated again. This cuts down on access time.

cartridge An early medium for the delivery of video games. From the late 1970s to mid-1990s, the majority of home video game systems were cartridge-based.

central processing unit (CPU) A single chip, such as a microprocessor, or a series of chips that performs arithmetic and logical calculations, and that times and controls the operations of the other elements of the system.

color depth The amount of space required to store the color of each pixel in an image.

compatibility testing The process of testing a particular game across all of the different configurations of hardware, peripherals and systems.

compiler A computer program that transforms source code written in one computer language (called the source language) into another computer language (called the target language).

concern A particular set of behaviors needed by a computer program. A concern can be as general as database interaction or as specific as performing a calculation.

console A video or computer game system that is hooked up to a television screen. Examples include the Nintendo Wii, the Sony PlayStation, and the Microsoft Xbox.

controller An input device used to control a video game. A controller is typically connected to a video game console or a personal computer. It can be a keyboard, mouse, gamepad, joystick, paddle, or any other device designed for gaming that can receive input. Special-purpose devices, such as steering wheels for driving games and light guns for shooting games, may also exist for a platform.

creep Refers to a phenomenon in the development of a game in which objectives that were not initially part of the design "sneak" into the project. For example, if one of the initial objectives of an adventure game was that the player could explore regions in 20 different countries around the globe and someone decides to increase that number to 30, that increase, small as it might seem, can overwhelm the resources already allotted to that portion of the project. This, in turn, could have a ripple effect in the project, causing critical deadlines to be missed, budgets to go over the mark, and even causing the project to ultimately fail.

cross-cutting concern Aspects of a program that affect other concerns. These concerns often cannot be easily broken down from the rest of the system in either design or implementation, and result in scattering or tangling of the program or both.

cut-scene A short, noninteractive scene in a game that displays narrative material. This scene is usually part of an ongoing storyline and appears between periods of game play. For example, once a player completes a level or a quest in a game, a cut-scene may appear directing the player where to go next or what the next quest will be.

d-pad The cross-shaped directional button on a controller.

data compression Also known as source coding, this is the process of encoding information using fewer bits than an unencoded representation would use through use of specific encoding schemes. Data compression is typically carried out by algorithms that find and remove redundancies in data.

debugger A programming tool that allows a programmer to monitor and modify a program as it runs.

demo With regard to animators, videographers, designers, and developers, this is a collection of a person's work that demonstrates his or her work experience and skills. It can include a portfolio of drawings, a computer program, an audio CD, or a DVD of animations, among other things.

dev station Also know as a dev bit, this is a collection of hardware and software tools that allows a programmer to create software for the game console. These are available only from the console manufacturer (which may be different from the company producing the game) and are only sold to licensed developers. They are akin to test machines used by software developers and testers in general.

digital This term refers to a computer system that uses discontinuous values, usually but not always symbolized numerically, to represent information for input, processing, transmission, storage, etc. By contrast, analog systems use a continuous range of values to represent information. Although digital representations are discrete, the information represented can be either discrete (numbers, letters, or icons) or continuous (sounds or images).

document object model A platform- and language-independent standard object model for representing HTML or XML documents as well as an application programming interface (API) for querying, traversing, and manipulating such documents.

driver A hardware device or program that controls or regulates another device. For example, a driver for a controller enables a computer and controller to communicate and work together.

dynamic range The range of loudness that can be represented by a certain number of data bits in terms of digital audio.

Easter egg A message, video, graphic, sound effect, or an unusual change in program behavior that sometimes occurs in a software program in response to an undocumented set of commands, mouse clicks, keystrokes, or other stimuli intended as a joke or to display program credits.

encryption The process of scrambling information for security purposes.

engine An aspect of a computer program that performs a particular task, often on an ongoing basis. Engines are typically reused in games, which saves on development costs. Examples include graphics engines and physics engines. The former

Professional
Ethics

Be honest and realistic when it comes to your capabilities and goals. One of the most common problems is to get halfway into a project and realize that you cannot complete it in the timeframe required. Perhaps the job was more complex than you originally thought, or unanticipated changes are required that affect other parts of the project, which now affects the ability to meet the deadline.

Rather than just working harder and hoping the project will be completed by some miracle, stop and think about the project goals. Why are they not being met? Talk to your team members. Brainstorm ideas and discuss which features can be left out or different ways to tackle the problem. Get together with everyone involved with the project and explain in detail the problem and your possible solutions. Most importantly, make sure a different approach is truly being taken to solve the problem. You will get nowhere fast if you keep trying to take the same approach, hoping for a different result.

display 3-D spaces on the screen, and the latter compute the behavior of moving objects.

executable file   The end product of the programming process. This is the file that is ready to be run on a computer or console for game play.

expansion pack   Additional content for a game that usually extends its life as a playable game. In other words, by purchasing an expansion pack for a game like *Zoo Tycoon*, users can explore new features, animals, settings, and so on not included with the original game.

fidget   Also referred to as idle animation, this is animation for a game character that is waiting around for something to do so that the character does not appear unnaturally still. For example, in *Sonic the Hedgehog*, if a player takes no action in the game for too long, Sonic will cross his arms and tap his foot impatiently.

firmware   Permanent commands, data, or programs that the computer needs to function correctly.

first party   A term that refers to a game that is developed by the same company who makes the console on which the game is played on—for example, Nintendo games for the Wii.

first person   A type of game play in which the action is seen through the character's viewpoint.

first-person shooter (FPS)   A shooting game with a first-person perspective.

force feedback   Technology that allows a controller—like a joystick or steering wheel, for example— to respond to the movement and signals in the game and respond accordingly. Examples include the recoil of a gun in a shooting game or the joystick shaking as the player tries to pull out of a crash.

frame buffer   An area of memory in which the image that will appear on the screen is rendered. Once all the data necessary is in the frame buffer, the graphics hardware displays the image on the screen.

frame rate   The rate at which a computer or other display system displays new frames on a screen, measured in frames per second. Because video games update the screen display at regular intervals, they have a frame rate. A high frame rate equals either fast code or fast hardware running the code.

function   Also known as a subroutine, this is the purpose of or action carried out by a program or routine.

geometry   A collective term for the polygons that make up a 3-D scene or model.

graphical user interface   A type of operating environment that represents programs, files, and options through the use of menus, icons, and dialog boxes. A user selects and activates these items by pointing and clicking with a mouse or using a keyboard.

hack   While the term often has nefarious connotations, with regards to video games it simply refers to creatively altering the behavior or an application or operating system by modifying its code rather than running the program and using it in the traditional manner.

hard drive   Also called a hard drive, this is a storage device on which data can be recorded magnetically.

hardware   The physical components of a computer system, such as printers, mice, keyboards, and the case. Also includes peripheral devices like joysticks, headsets, and external drives.

hit points   A numerical representation of a character's capacity for damage—that is, the character's health status or life remaining—frequently employed in role-playing games. Some games use colored bars or other graphic meters to indicate this.

index (v)   To create and use a list or table that contains reference information pointing to stored data; to locate information stored

INTERVIEW

Know Your Skill Level—and Then Take It Up a Notch

Harry Pehbianto
3-D Artist, Matahari Studios

How long have you been in this industry and what drew you to it?
I've been in the industry almost four years, having been interested in video games since I was a child. While my experience was initially in architectural design, I wanted to be in the gaming industry, so I learned 3-D software.

Have you seen the hot areas in this industry change over time or have they remained relatively the same? What are these hot areas in your opinion?
Well, some parts have changed quickly, like the graphics technology; others are staying relatively the same. I believe the way games will be played are going to start changing rapidly and will be a new hot area.

What new trends are you noticing?
This is the era of multimedia, where people can do almost anything with a single product. Take PlayStation 3, for example. We can do

in a table by adding an offset amount, called the index, to the base address of the table.

instance   In object-oriented programming, this is an object in relation to the class in which it belongs. An instance may contain data or instructions.

integrated development environment (IDE)   An application that combines an editor, compiler, linker, debugger, and so on into a single tool so that work can be carried out in one application instead of switching back and forth between several.

interactive   A game is interactive when it requires the actions or input of a user in order to function.

joystick   A means of controlling game play, this device resembles an airplane's joystick and is capable of motion in two or more directions.

almost anything with that. We can chat, play games, watch movies, play music, use WiFi technology, share files.

While there is no formal "career plan" per se, in this field, how does one go about planning a career in video games?
The first thing—perhaps the most important thing—is to know your skill level. Do not ever dream you can do it all by yourself. That will confuse you and bog you down. However, do not be afraid to take on a challenge. It will hone your skills quickly. Mentors are recommended, as they can guide you and help you make the right choices.

What do you consider the biggest myth about the video game industry, if any?
I think a lot of people think video games are just for kids and are not suitable for adults. But the fact is that adults play video games and a lot of the games available today are made for a mature audience—like *Grand Theft Auto IV*. It rocks!

Is there anything else a person new to this industry should know?
Creating games, while fun, is not as much fun as playing games. This job can certainly be fun, but effort and hard work is very much a part of the process. And you need to know what you are doing. Be skillful, be creative, and if you do not know how to do something, ask. Do not just guess.

kernel   The core of an operating system. It manages memory, files, and peripheral devices; maintains the time and date; launches applications; and allocates system resources.

kilobyte   A unit of data consisting of 1,024 bytes. Often abbreviated as K, KB, or Kbyte.

kinematics   A computer animation technique in which the computer calculates the position of a creature's arms, legs, head, and so on with each step or action it takes.

language   A specific pattern of binary digital information.

launch   To release a game to the public for purchase and use.

lifecycle   The stages a game goes through, from the initial concept, to development, to testing, to release.

linker   A tool that binds different modules of a program together into a single executable file.

local area network (LAN) A group of computers and other devices dispersed over a relatively small area and connected by a link that enables devices and computers to communicate with one another.

localization Enabling a game to be sold in another country by changing the text and language—and sometimes the code and graphics as well (from a vertical to horizontal orientation, for example)—to the language of the destination country (or countries).

logarithm The exponent that indicates the power to which a base number is raised to produce a given number. For example, the logarithm of 1,000 to the base 10 is 3, because you must multiply 10 by 3 to get 1,000—thus $10 \_ 10 \_ 10 = 1000$. Computer languages such as C and BASIC include functions for calculating natural algorithms.

lossless compression A data-compression technique that preserves all data, enabling it to be decompressed back into a file identical to the original.

lossy compression A data-compression technique that results in some information being irretrievably lost. Lossy compression may be used when this loss of information is not significant—for example, in video or audio, where the missing data is not likely to be noticed.

machine code A system of instructions and data executed directly by a computer's central processing unit

memory A device where information can be stored and retrieved. This may be a tape drive or a disk drive (external devices), or the RAM that is connected directly to the computer.

method In object-oriented programming, this is a process performed by an object when it receives a message.

microprocessor Also called the central processing unit (CPU), this is the device that interprets and carries out instructions—in other words, it is the "brain" of the computer.

middleware Computer software that connects other software components or applications. It includes Web servers, application servers, and similar tools that support application development and delivery. This prewritten software can help cut the development time of a game significantly.

MIP mapping An approach to texture mapping in which an original high-resolution texture map is scaled and filtered into multiple resolutions before it is applied to a surface. (MIP stands for the Latin multim im parvo, meaning "many things in a small space.") When the camera is far away, for example, a lower-resolution texture is displayed; a high-resolution texture is used in a close-up scene.

MMOG (massively multiplayer online game)   A game played over the Internet by hundreds, possibly even thousands, of people at the same time. MMORPGs (massively multiplayer online role-playing games) deal specifically with role-playing games and character development through combat, quests, etc. Examples include *EverQuest*, *World of Warcraft*, and the *Final Fantasy* series.

MOO (MUD, object-oriented)   An interactive, virtual community in which members can communicate via text-based commands.

motherboard   The main circuit board of a computer, containing the primary components of the system: the processor, main memory, bus controller, connector, and support circuitry.

motion capture   A technique for converting the motion of actual objects (typically people) into data that is then turned into animations, generally by using 3-D models. This technique is frequently used on athletes for sports games, martial artists for combat games, and actors and actresses for games based on popular movies or TV shows.

MUD (multiuser dungeon)   A multiuser, real-time virtual world described entirely in text. It combines elements of role-playing games, combat, interactive fiction, and online chat. Players can read descriptions of rooms, objects, other players, nonplayer characters, and actions performed in the virtual world. Players interact with each other and the world by typing commands that resemble a natural language. Most MUDs are noncommercial, built by hobbyists, and cost nothing to play.

multimedia   The combination of sound, graphics, and video. This can also refer to a subset of hypermedia, which combines these elements with hypertext.

multiprocessing   The use of two or more central processing units within a single computer system. Also, to the ability of a system to support more than one processor and/or the ability to allocate tasks between them. The objective in any case is increased speed and computing power.

INTERVIEW

The Importance of Passion

Ramadona Samita
Art Outsourcing Manager, Matahari Studios

How long have you been in this industry? What was your introduction to it?
I've been in the industry for five years. Art and video games have drawn my interest since a young age, but seeing a poster for a local game developer seminar introduced me to the opportunity of making a living in the game industry. I started out as a freelance interactive multimedia designer creating art and programming assets for educational games. These provided me with the basic experience and knowledge of the production pipeline. And the rest is history.

What are the hot areas in this industry as you see them?
I believe creativity, technology, the Internet, and the players are the hot areas in this industry. [This] has always been a creative industry. Creativity ignites innovations. Technology and the Internet provide the platform to harness [these innovations]. And by the end of the development days, the players [are the ones] who determine and provide feedback on whether a game is good or not and gets the business, and then the industry, rolling.

What trends have you noticed as far as job opportunities? Can you predict any new trends?
I see the connection between games, movies, and merchandizing [coming together more]. The rapid evolution of tools and technology

multitasking   The ability of a computer system to work on more than one task at a time.

natural language   Any language that is spoken, signed, or written by humans for general-purpose communication. Compare to computer language, which is a machine-readable artificial language designed to express computations that can be performed by a machine, namely, a computer.

nonplayer character (NPC)   A character that is controlled by the game system via the computer rather than by the player.

makes development a lot easier as we move forward and opens up new opportunities. Also, as modern society evolves, mobile and networking development trends seems to be the most surprising for me, as they open up another whole new world for game development and its market.

What strengths/talents do you think make someone well suited for the video game industry?
The ability to be part of a team, good communication, a drive for competitiveness and the willingness to strive for continuous improvement, and most importantly, the passion to fit all this into an exciting and productive working environment.

What is the most important thing someone needs to know who is considering entering the video game industry today?
You must have passion. The video game industry is fast-evolving—new tools, game engines, genres, platforms, pipelines—these all come up so quickly as technology provides more room for creativity to be brought to life. You just must have passion for this industry to keep up with this rhythm.

Is there anything a person new to this industry should know?
Creating games is often not much as fun as playing them. With long hours of tweaking and improvement, you might easily get lost—unless you have the passion. For those who choose to be a game artist, as much as you need to understand and be able to work with the latest digital tools, traditional media, such as drawing, sculpting, and painting, among others, is still the solid foundation of all digital art.

object file   The output of a compiler or assembler, this file contains machine code, but cannot be run by a computer until it is linked to other object files and forms an executable file.

object-oriented programming   In terms of software, a program is viewed as a collection of discrete objects that are themselves collections of self-contained collections of data structures that interact with other objects.

open-source (adj)   In reference to computer programming, this term refers to the free exchange and collaboration of developers and producers. The definition put forth by Bruce Perens, a well-known computer programmer, is widely recognized as the "real" definition: "A broad, general type of software license that makes source code available to the general public with relaxed or nonexistent copyright restrictions."

oscilloscope   A type of electronic test instrument that allows signal voltages to be viewed, usually as a two-dimensional graph of one or more electrical potential differences (on the vertical axis) plotted as a function of time or of some other voltage (on the horizontal axis).

packet   A unit of information that is transmitted in its entirety from one device to another on a network.

patch   Downloadable software that fixes bugs or adds features to a game after it has already shipped.

peripheral device   An ancillary device connected to a computer and controlled by it. Examples include (but are not limited to) speakers, joysticks, paddles, keyboards, mice, modems, and printers.

pipeline   An automated process whereby a designer or artist inserts assets into a game without sending it to the programmer to insert. This tool is often used with data that occurs repeatedly throughout a game—for example, an explosion every time a bomb is detonated. Once the pipeline tool is built (and debugged), it can go to the programmer for further development.

pixel   The smallest unit of information in an image.

platform   As it pertains to computers, this term refers to a hardware architecture or software framework (including application frameworks) that allows software to run. Typical platforms include a computer's architecture, operating system, programming languages, and related runtime libraries or graphical user interface.

player character   The character controlled by the player.

polygon   The basic building block of data displayed by a 3-D graphics engine. The term refers to a region of 3-D space described by three or four points, called vertices, which are linked to form triangle or quadrilateral, respectively. Three-dimensional models consist of hundreds—often thousands—polygons linked together to create a surface. The speed at which 3-D acceleration hardware is measure is referred to as polygons per second.

Fast Facts

So what was the first computer game? To some, the first computer game was not *Spacewar* or *Tennis for Two*. Technically, the world's first computer game was an automated chess game called *El Ajedrecista* (*The Chessplayer*). The game, which was invented by Spanish engineer and mathematician Gonzales Torres y Quevedos in early 1910, was able to automatically play a king and rook endgame against a king from any position, without any human intervention. This device was first publicly demonstrated in Paris in 1914, and mechanical arms moved the pieces in the prototype. By 1920, electromagnets under the board were employed for this task.

port   A later version of a game that has been revised so that it can work on a system different from the one for which it was originally intended.

portfolio   A collection of materials that are representative of a person's work. A designer, for example, may have a portfolio of demos from games that he has worked on. An animator may have drawings of characters for a video game that she has brought to life.

processor   Also called the central processing unit (CPU), this is the device that interprets and carries out instructions—in other words, it is the "brain" of the computer.

profiler   Also called a performance analyzer, this tool helps identify where a program is spending its time so that slow routines can be identified and resolved.

program   A sequence of instructions that tells the hardware of a computer what operations to perform on data.

render   To produce an image on scene by converting the data that represents the scene geometry.

résumé   A document outlining a person's job history, duties, responsibilities, publications, and other achievements.

role-playing game (RPG)   A game in which the player assumes the role of a character (or characters). These games usually take place in a fantasy setting and players engage on various quests.

routine   Any section of code that can be executed within a program.

royalties   Any payment that is received as a percentage of the revenue generated by the sale of something. For example, author Tom Clancy likely receives royalties on the popular *Rainbow Six* series of video games based on his novel of the same name. Development companies receive royalties from the publisher on the wholesale sales of a game that they develop.

save point   A predetermined place in the game where the player can choose to save game progress in order to return to it at a later time. Some games create save points automatically.

shelf life   The amount of time that a game remains in stores, available for purchase.

ship date   The day that the completed game physically leaves the manufacturing or distribution facility and is sent to retailers.

SKU   Pronounced "skew," this is a game released for a specific hardware and operating system combination. For example, a typical game might have a separate version for PCs, Mac, Xbox, and PlayStation, each of which represents a different SKU.

slate   A list of overview of all the games a publisher intends to release in the future.

software   Computer programs or instructions that make hardware work. In general, software can be thought of as one of two types. System software refers to a computer's operating system. Applications perform the tasks for which people use computers—for example, word processing programs, spreadsheet programs, databases—and games!

software toy   A video game without a well-defined, specific goal (a victory condition). While such games are played largely for fun, some do have challenges to overcome and problems to solve. Examples of software toys include *Marble Drop*, *Railroad Tycoon*, *Creatures*, and the *Petz* series.

sold-in   The number of units of a game that have been sold to the retailer by publishers but not necessarily purchased by consumers.

sold-through   The number of units of a game that have been bought by consumers from retailers.

spawn (n)   The reappearance of a dead character or defeated enemy.

sprite   A small 2-D image of an object or character that can be drawn on the screen at different locations over time to give the illusion of movement. Associated movements include walking, jumping, shooting, and so on.

storyboard   A graphic organization of the progression of a visual display of some kind, whether it be animation, a particular camera shot, motion graphic, or multimedia sequence.

subroutine   Another word for routine; however, it usually refers to sections of code that are short and called on a more frequent basis.

system   At its most basic level, any grouping of components that work together to perform a task are functioning as a system. A hardware system, for example, consists of the microprocessor, computer chips, circuitry, peripheral devices, and input and output devices. An operating system consists of program files, data files, and other applications used to process information.

texel   A pixel that is part of a texture.

text editor   Typically used for editing program code, this device often contains built-in features to help prevent a programmer from introducing syntax errors into the code.

texture   A 2-D surface that is mapped onto the surface of a polygon in a 3-D environment in order to create the appearance of a surface. For example, the fur on a minotaur in a fantasy game is created using a texture. The minotaur is the 3-D shape, with the texture creating the fur mapped onto it.

third party   A term that describes a game that is developed by one company for another company's hardware—for example, Sega. While the company started out producing both consoles and games, it eventually settled on becoming a third-party manufacturer of games for other consoles.

tilting   The act of tipping or otherwise moving a pinball machine to affect game play.

touchscreen   A device that senses a touch and its location on a screen—usually with a finger or stylus—and carries out requested actions as a result.

transistor   A solid-state circuit component with at least three terminals in which a voltage or current controls the flow of another current. A transistor is commonly used to amplify a signal, and is the fundamental building block of computers, radios, phones, and other electronic devices.

unlock   To access part of a game or an item in a game that was previously unavailable. This can be accomplished by achieving a certain number of points, completing a certain level, or when other criteria are fulfilled.

victory condition   The goal of a video game. This is usually quite specific in nature and well defined. For example, in *Donkey Kong*, the victory goal in each level is to reach the top of the tower and free the girl.

Chapter 6

Resources

This book was designed to be as comprehensive a guide as possible for those launching a career in the video game field. However, this book can only contain so much information, and some areas, while certainly interesting, are beyond the scope of this book. The sections in this chapter provide sources of more information, ranging from books and periodicals to Web sites, schools, training programs, and more.

Associations and Organizations

While gaming itself is a social endeavor and often provides players with an instant community—especially for those who play games online—joining a professional association can help you build a professional reputation early on in your career. Membership in such an organization shows that while you like to have fun in your work, you understand the serious nature behind it, too, and desire to further your career knowledge. As with many fields, networking—that is, who you know and who knows you—is critical. Not all jobs are posted publicly, and the right word in someone's ear could land you that key position you have been working so hard to achieve. Coworkers or mentors can advise you (and perhaps even sponsor you, if need be) as to what organizations and associations are of the most benefit.

Professional Organizations

Academy of Interactive Arts and Sciences   This organization is aimed at promoting and leading the interactive software industry. Members of the board of directors include Jay Cohen, President of Development, Jerry Bruckheimer Games; Rich Hilleman, Electronic Arts; Don James, Nintendo of America; and Josh Resnick, President and Co-founder, Pandemic Studios. This nonprofit organization was founded in 1996, and its annual DICE Summit event (see chapter 2) is where its Interactive Achievement Awards ceremony has been held annually since 1998. AIAS membership consists of industry professionals, and only professional members who meet a set of minimum criteria are able to vote for the best entertainment software of the year. (http://www.interactive.org)

Association for the Advancement of Artificial Intelligence   The AAAI is a nonprofit scientific society devoted to "advancing the scientific understanding of the mechanisms underlying thought and intelligent behavior and their embodiment in machines. AAAI also aims to increase public understanding of artificial intelligence, improve the teaching and training of AI practitioners, and provide guidance for research planners and funders concerning the importance and potential of current AI developments and future directions." (http://www.aaai.org/home.html)

Association for Computing and Machinery   This group touts itself as "the premier membership organization for computing professionals, delivering resources that advance computing as a science and a profession; enable professional development; and promote policies and research that benefit society." People looking to launch a career in this field may find the Career and Job Center particularly useful. (http://www.acm.org)

Association for Multimedia Communications   This is an organization that "promotes understanding of technology, e-learning, and e-business." Part of the organization's mission is to help member achieve success in their chosen field. They do this by offering education and networking opportunities. Members also can search for job opportunities. (http://www.amcomm.org)

Association for Women in Computing   This national, nonprofit, professional organization is designed to "promote awareness on issues affecting women in the computing industry, further the professional development and advancement of women in computing, and encourage women to enter computing as a career." Information on scholarships, a job network, and regular community events are also included. The link cited here is for the Puget Sound chapter, but chapters are available throughout the United States. (http://www.awcps.org)

The Interactive Digital Software Association IDSA is dedicated to serving the business and public affairs needs of companies that publish video and computer games for video game consoles, personal computers, and the Internet. IDSA offers services to interactive entertainment software publishers, including a global anti-piracy program, owning the Electronic Entertainment Expo (E3) trade show, business and consumer research, government relations, and First Amendment and intellectual property protection efforts. (http://www.idsa.com)

International Game Developers' Association This organization is one of the most important sites for in the world of game development, and the organization's mission is "to advance the careers and enhance the lives of game developers by connecting members with their peers, promoting professional development, and advocating on issues that affect the developer community." To that end, the organization provides extensive networking opportunities through its chapter groups, events and parties, and

Fast Facts

An Easter egg is a message that is intentionally hidden in a video game. It may be a credits list of everyone who worked on the game, an in-joke, a bonus level or game, a video clip—the possibilities are nearly endless. According to programmer and founder of The Learning Company Warren Robinett, the term was coined by Atari after they were alerted to the secret message Robinett left in the game *Adventure*. However, evidence of Easter eggs predating this one has since come to light. And Easter eggs are not just limited to video games: consider Alfred Hitchcock's legendary cameo appearances in his movies and the various "hidden Mickeys" that can be found throughout Disneyland.

forums; offers professional development and educational programs; and provides standards and guidelines that help shape the
industry and move it forward, among other things. (http://www
.igda.org)

Books and Periodicals

The list of items provided here is by no means exhaustive. Rather,
it is designed to provide a jumping-off point, and one book or peri-
odical may take two readers in two different directions. Check out
your favorite online bookstore and see what recommendations others have.

It should come as no surprise that there are fewer hard-copy
magazines and journals these days—most are available online. However, even the print versions have a Web site, with access to archived
issues, reviews, discussion groups—and job boards, in some cases.
Anyone looking to advance their career would be wise to subscribe
to these or other periodicals and read them faithfully. Coworkers
can also provide reading suggestions.

Books

The A-Z of Cool Computer Games. By Jack Railton (Allison & Busby,
   2005). This comprehensive guid provides an alphabetical listing
   of the coolest games, starting with the 1970s and ending with the
   PlayStation. The book is written in an engaging, witty style, and
   includes things that you might not ordinarily think of when it
   comes to computer games, such as pocket calculators.
*Dungeons and Desktops: The History of Computer Role-Playing
   Games*. By Matt Barton (AK Peters, 2008). This book provides
   a detailed overview of the history of RPGs, from the early rough
   days to today's slick, widely popular titles that will appeal to both
   hardcore gamers and casual players alike.
The Elements of Style. By William Strunk and E.B. White (Pen-
   guin, 2007). Strunk and White's book is a timeless classic that
   serves as an invaluable reference guide for how to write clearly
   and succinctly—for those both in and out of the computer field.
   It explains basic principles of grammar in plain English and—
   interestingly enough—is the only style guide to have appeared
   on the best-seller lists.

Game Boys. By Michael Kane (Viking, 2008). An engrossing look at the rise of professional video gaming, this book examines the trials and tribulations, the princes and the primadonnas, the battles for dominance, and how the sport of video gaming is becoming just as competitive, lucrative, and controversial as any other type of professional sport.

Game Over: Press Continue to Start. By David Sheff and Andy Eddy (Cyberactive Media Group, 1999). This volume focuses on the history of Nintendo, from its beginning as a playing card manufacturer to its rise in the annals of video game history. And the authors do not shy away from the messy details, discussing at length Nintendo's legal battles with Atari and Sega as the company battled for industry leadership.

Best Practice

In order to get the most out of your career and see it truly move forward, make sure each assignment has something new in it. It may seem obvious, but in a ten-year career, for example, you want ten years of experience, not one year of experience ten times.

Occupational Outlook Handbook, 2008-09 Edition, Computer Support Specialists and Systems Administrators. By the Bureau of Labor Statistics, U.S. Department of Labor (Government-Issued). In this handbook, readers can find more detailed information on the typical working environment for the positions described in this book, related occupations, additional data on projections and outlook, and more.

Power-up: How Japanese Video Games Gave the World an Extra Life. By Chris Kohler (BradyGames, 2005). Kohler's work makes a compelling case for the pivotal role Japan played in the history of video games, helping to resurrect the industry when both sales and interest waned. Whether you are a die-hard fan of Mario and Zelda or just interested in Japanese culture (there is a section on shopping in Akihabara, a famous area with plenty of electronics shops), this book is an entertaining read.

Trigger Happy: Videogames and the Entertainment Revolution. By Steven Poole (Arcade Publishing, 2004). Though it does provide a history of the video game industry, the focus is on the esthetics of gaming and how that helps effect what makes a game great as opposed to "just okay." Topics include what features work better in some genres than in others, why we respond to certain games more than others, and how our personal experiences play a role in how we respond to games. If you are a fan of both video games and philosophy, this is the book for you.

The Ultimate History of Video Games. By Steven L. Kent (Prima Publishing, 2001). This book provides a vast, wide-ranging look at video games, from the early days of *Spacewar* to Wii—and beyond. If you are interested in learning more about the history of this field after reading chapter 1, this book is a wonderful place to dive in.

Periodicals

1Up.com   This is the reincarnation of *Electronic Gaming Monthly* and provides video game reviews, cheats, hacks, and message boards, among other features. The site is comprehensive and easy to navigate, and includes blogs written by developers and users. (http://www.1up.com/do/pubs?did=2)

BusinessWeek   It may not seem particularly relevant at first glance to someone new to the video game field; however, with articles on technology, investing, companies, innovation, and more, the astute person may, just by paying a little attention, identify upcoming trends in this industry and take advantage of them. (http://www.businessweek.com)

Edge   This is an online magazine with a broad-spectrum take on the video game industry. It includes previews of upcoming games, reviews of recently released titles, opinion columns, in-depth features, and more. (http://www.edge-online.com)

PC Gamer   This magazine is available in both print and online forms. It provides reviews, how-to articles on systems and hardware, gaming news, previews, and more. (http://www.pcgamer.com)

Wired   Available in both print and online forms, *Wired* reports on how technology affects culture, the economy, and politics. (http://www.wired.com)

Web Sites

The sites included here complement the associations, organizations, books, and periodicals listed above, and will give the motivated career launcher a complete picture of the video game industry.

AllConferences.com This site provides a comprehensive list of computer-related conferences. Areas of focus include artificial intelligence, databases, mobile computing, open source, security, virtual reality, and more. (http://www.allconferences.com/Computers)

Gamasutra Developed and hosted by the same company behind the Game Developers Conference and *Game Developer* magazine, this is the go-to site for anyone who works in the video game industry—or for people who just really, really love them. The site include columns and blogs, contractors available for work by category, and a résumé database and job board. (http://www.gamasutra.com)

GameFAQs This is a comprehensive site aimed to help people both understand and play games better. The site contains reviews, contests, project stats, and brief overviews of the companies behind the games and platforms discussed on the site. The most important feature of the site, however, is the extensive collection of FAQs (frequently asked questions). If you are stuck and need help getting through a game, this is the site for you. You can also see a list of the games that still need a FAQ. Write one, and you could win a gift certificate for a new game. (http://www.gamefaqs.com)

The Games List Billed as "the world's greatest social networking site for casual gaming," this site offers hundreds of games and asks readers to rate the games once they've played them. As a result, when you return to the site, you will receive game recommendations based on your preferences. Members are encouraged to add games for others to play and rate. (http://www.thegameslist.com)

Gamespot This is another great, well-rounded site for gaming fans. The site includes news articles, reviews on games and game systems, downloads, hints, and more. Visitors can even watch video clips of games and comment on them. (http://www.gamespot .com)

Inside Mac Games This site addresses that special niche market—video games for the Mac. It may seem that this operating system gets overlooked in the crush of PC and console games available. However, developers and publishers know better than to ignore this chunk of the market. This long-running site contains news on upcoming releases, reviews of current games, general videogame news, and more. (http://www.insidemacgames.com)

The Killer List of Videogames An offshoot of The International Arcade Museum, this is a searchable database of more than 4,000 games. Want to learn more about coin-operated games, slot machines, or pinball machines? This is the place to go. The site also contains message boards, a gift shop, a list of upcoming events, and more. (http://www.klov.com)

MobyGames Comparable to the Internet Movie Database, but for video games, visitors to the site can find out the most minute details of games, including general descriptions, press reviews, user reviews, trivia, credits, technical specifications, and more. There are also in-depth reviews written by highly knowledgeable community members. (http://www.mobygames.com)

Steam This is the site for game developer Valve, through which games are distributed online. Visitors can find not only Valve's games, but also games from publishers like Rockstar, Sega, and Ubisoft. What makes this site unique is that games receive patches

Problem
Solving

Despite everyone's best efforts, from time to time it happens: A game is released to customers, who then discover a problem. Perhaps a feature does not work the way it is supposed to or there are problems downloading and installing the game. For example, in 1994, the Walt Disney Corporation, seeking to capitalize on its mega-hit movie *The Lion King*, decided to release a PC video game just in time for Christmas. At the same time, the "Multimedia PC standard" was introduced. This was a PC with an 808486 processer, an 8-bit Sound Blaster card, and a single-speed CD-ROM drive. Millions of these machines were purchased in the belief that they were the latest and greatest next evolution of the PC. The problem? Someone at Disney had decided that *The Lion King* game would sound better in a 16-bit sound card, and that was the machine they developed it for. Thus, on Christmas morning, Disney's help desk lines were jammed with calls from irate parents demanding to know why the game would not work on their Multimedia PC. More than half of the games were returned.

The lesson? Configuration tests must be conducted on all sorts of machines. In addition, when such problems do occur (and they are common), it is important to address the issue as quickly as possible, provide a fix to players as quickly as possible (this was not possible with the Disney scenario), and document the problem internally to ensure that it does not happen again.

(or updates) automatically and can be played on any PC with broadband Internet access. (http://www.steampowered.com)

What They Play This site is a valuable resource for parents who want to know what their kids are playing and whether these games are truly suitable for them. The site goes beyond the ESRB ratings, with in-depth reviews and analysis of content, feature articles, blogs, and lists of the most popular games according to rating. (http://www.whattheyplay.com)

Educational Institutions

While some people certainly manage to have a successful career in the video game industry without any formal schooling or training, those people are few and far between. As interview candidates have emphasized throughout this book, just because you love video games and can play them well, this does not necessarily make you well suited for a career in this field. Training and schooling are necessary—if not to land that first job, then at the very least to see your career move forward. The schools described in this section offer either full degree programs or multiple courses in game design. However, this list is by no means exhaustive. Readers are encouraged to contact the schools directly for more information.

Art Center College of Design Located in Pasadena, California, this school offers undergraduate and graduate degrees in a wide range of areas, from advertising and entertainment design, to digital media and graphic design. (http://www.artcenter.edu)

The Art Institute The Art Institute has locations throughout the United States, and classes are conducted both in physical classrooms and online. For the video game enthusiast areas of study include game design and programming; animation and special effects; audio, video, or film production; and Web design and interactive media. (http://www.artinstitutes.edu)

Carnegie Mellon University With its main location in Pittsburgh, Pennsylvania, CMU maintains satellite campuses throughout the world. The school consists of seven schools and colleges: Carnegie Institute of Technology, College of Fine Arts, College of Humanities and Social Sciences, Heinz College, Mellon College of Science, School of Computer Science and the Tepper School of Business. The university has been endorsed by characters on *Buffy the Vampire Slayer* and *The West Wing*; spoofed by *The Muppets*;

and scenes from the movies *Smart People, The Mothman Prophecies, Wonder Boys, Dogma,* and *Flashdance* were filmed on campus. (http://www.cmu.edu)

DigiPen Institute of Technology This institute is located in Redmond, Washington, and offers both undergraduate and graduate programs. The school is focused entirely on making games, unlike other schools and colleges mentioned in this section. It also offers two-week exploratory workshops for students in grade five and higher, comprehensive high school programs at locations across the United States and in Canada, and continuing education opportunities for industry professionals. The school was actually created to fill a need for qualified, talented professionals in computer simulation and animation, and was developed as a result of collaboration between Nintendo and Claude Comair of DigiPen Corporation. (http://www.digipen.edu)

Full Sail University Full Sail offers undergraduate and graduate courses in a wide range of areas, such as game design, computer animation, game art, game development, graphic design, and the entertainment industry. Located in Winter Park, Florida, courses are generally four weeks long—and they are intense. Graduates from the school have gone on to work on games such as *Call of Duty, Tom Clancy's Ghost Recon,* and *Resistance.* (http://www.fullsail.edu)

According to the *U.S. News & World Report* 2009 survey, the best colleges to obtain an undergraduate degree in computer engineering, where the highest degrees offered are a bachelor's or master's are:

➡ Rose-Hulman Institute of Technology, Terre Haute, IN (http://www.rose-hulman.edu)
➡ Cal Poly-San Luis Obispo, San Luis Obispo, CA (http://www.calpoly.edu)
➡ Harvey Mudd College, Claremont, CA (http://www.hmc.edu)
➡ Cooper Union, New York, NY (http://www.cooper.edu)
➡ San Jose State University, San Jose, CA (http://www.sjsu.edu)
➡ Bucknell University, Lewisburg, PA (http://www.bucknell.edu)

The best colleges to obtain an undergraduate degree in computer engineering where the highest degree offered is a doctorate include:

➡ Massachusetts Institute of Technology, Cambridge, MA
   (http://web.mit.edu)
➡ Stanford University, Stanford, CA
   (http://www.stanford.edu)
➡ Carnegie Mellon University, Pittsburgh, PA
   (http://www.cmu.edu)
➡ University of California-Berkeley, Berkeley, CA
   (http://www.berkeley.edu)
➡ University of Illinois-Urbana-Champaign, Champaign, IL
   (http://www.uiuc.edu)
➡ Georgia Institute of Technology, Atlanta, GA
   (http://www.gatech.edu/welcome)
➡ University of Michigan-Ann Arbor, Ann Arbor, MI
   (http://www.umich.edu)
➡ California Institute of Technology, Pasadena, CA
   (http://www.caltech.edu)
➡ Cornell University, Ithaca, NY
   (http://www.cornell.edu)
➡ University of Texas-Austin, Austin, TX
   (http://www.utexas.edu)

U.S. News & World Report states that rankings of undergraduate programs accredited by the Accreditation Board for Engineering and Technology are "based solely on the judgments of deans and senior faculty, who rated each program they are familiar with on a scale from 1 (marginal) to 5 (distinguished)." There are separate rankings for colleges that offer doctoral degrees and those whose highest degree is a bachelor's or master's because "[r]esearch at the graduate level often influences the undergraduate curriculum, and schools with doctoral programs in engineering tend to have the widest possible range of offerings." While the focus of these lists was computer engineering, these schools also offer programs that can be of use to video game developers and others in this field.

Index